PROFILING THE
LETHAL EMPLOYEE

PROFILING THE LETHAL EMPLOYEE

Case Studies of Violence in the Workplace

MICHAEL D. KELLEHER

Westport, Connecticut
London

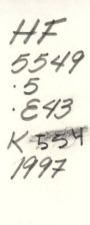

Library of Congress Cataloging-in-Publication Data

Kelleher, Michael D.
    Profiling the lethal employee : case studies of violence in
the workplace / Michael D. Kelleher.
        p.   cm.
    Includes bibliographical references and index.
    ISBN 0–275–95756–X (alk. paper)
    1. Violence in the workplace—Prevention.   2. Criminals—
Psychology.   3. Violence in the workplace—United States—Case
studies.   I. Title.
HF5549.5.E43K448   1997
658.4′73—DC20   96–26280

British Library Cataloguing in Publication Data is available.

Library of Congress Catalog Card Number: 96–26280
ISBN: 0–275–95756–X

First published in 1997

Praeger Publishers, 88 Post Road West, Westport, CT 06881
An imprint of Greenwood Publishing Group, Inc.

Printed in the United States of America

The paper used in this book complies with the
Permanent Paper Standard issued by the National
Information Standards Organization (Z39.48–1984).

10 9 8 7 6 5 4 3 2

For Cindy

Contents

Illustrations

Introduction

One of the emerging areas of major crime in the United States is occupational homicide—murder in the workplace. Many jobs in this country are inherently dangerous, such as those in law enforcement or security; the possibility of being murdered at work is direct and ever-present for employees in these professions. Indirectly, however, large numbers of other workers in such segments of the economy as the retail trades are at risk because of the pervasive threats of robbery, extortion or other confrontational crimes. Few Americans are surprised to learn of a police officer murdered on the job or a store clerk shot to death in a convenience store robbery. These violent crimes have become commonplace; the perpetrators and their methods are generally known. Their motivations, although heinous, are generally understood.

In the past decade, however, a new criminal has made his mark on the American business community. He is the lethal employee—a murderer who strikes exclusively at his coworkers, and typically, with horrendous results. He may target a supervisor or member of management against whom he holds a grudge but is just as likely to murder fellow employees or clients, seemingly at random. In fact, he often appears to kill indiscriminately. Sometimes, in a final act of desperation, he will take his own life along with those of his victims.

This perpetrator is unlike others who prey openly upon the workplace because he is a *member* of the workforce. In this sense, he has the perfect cover. He is usually over thirty and sometimes middle-aged. Most likely, he has never committed a major crime in his life prior to his murderous rampage. He may have worked for an organization for several years—perhaps decades—before victimizing it. Frequently, he is still on the job the day he begins his murder spree or may have just been fired and is returning to the job site for a final time. His obvious advantage is that he is known to his coworkers—he is not seriously considered to be a potential murderer, yet he may be deadly serious about revenge.

This murderer-in-waiting may live in relative comfort and, in most respects, may conform to the accepted norms of society. He may be thought of as a good neighbor by those who live nearby; or, perhaps, may be considered a harmless loner. Sometimes he is the financial support for other family members, and perhaps even a successful father and husband. However, in what is typically just a few moments of chaos, he will be reborn as a destroyer of life more ruthless than the majority of convenience store robbers or police killers. He will commonly murder at least two individuals—and sometimes many more—before he is finished. His actions can result in mass murder.

Even more frightening than the violent eruption of his rampage is the evidence that the lethal employee is becoming a more frequent killer as the new millennium approaches. He is carrying out his mayhem across America with greater vehemence and destruction, and with increasing frequency, yet he often remains unseen and unrecognized until it is too late. It is difficult, if not impossible, to know where he will strike next and how many victims he will leave behind. What is certain is that the lethal employee has already victimized a wide range of work environments throughout this nation and will continue to do so unless the business community is provided with an effective means of prevention.

Occupational homicide in the United States is an emerging issue of troublesome proportions. What has been learned about this crime has been derived primarily from a history of violent incidents in the workplace. What is known about the perpetrator and his motives is often sketchy and sometimes entirely absent. This crime is not often addressed by organizational prevention programs, despite the fact it is a clear and increasing threat to many work environments. Nonlethal workplace violence, which is sometimes the precursor to workplace homicide, is just now beginning to receive the serious attention of some organizational managers and, thankfully, it is increasingly being perceived as a crucial issue in many forward-looking safety programs. Although this is a positive indicator of a commitment to employee wellness, it comes at a time when general workplace violence is epidemic, impacting some one million workers each year. It would be unthinkable to delay addressing the specific issue of workplace homicide until it reaches a similar level of devastation in the U.S. business community.

The American workforce is in need of methods to protect itself against the mayhem and death that can be wrought on it in such a senseless and seemingly unpredictable manner. Crucial to constructing such a method of protection is gaining an understanding of the crime and, of most importance, the behavior of the potentially violent individual before he has become committed to violent action. Occupational homicide cannot be resolved after the crime has been committed. The most effective form of protection implies the ability to recognize a potentially lethal situation and take action to intervene before it escalates. This requires the skill to recognize the emerging signs of aggression within an individual before he becomes violent and, certainly, before he becomes lethal. The American workforce can no longer assume a safe working environment, nor can it rely on overburdened law enforcement agencies to protect its members. Whatever action is to be taken to protect the workforce must be taken in the workplace by concerned employees and supervisors.

It may prove comforting to dismiss the threat of occupational homicide as insignificant on a personal level. One could argue that the odds of being struck by lightning are greater than those of being murdered by a coworker. Depending upon the statistical model you choose, this could be true—for today. However, the odds of being struck by lightning have not changed significantly in the past few decades, while the odds of being murdered on the job have skyrocketed. Perhaps it would be wise not to rely on the current odds as any guarantee of safety.

Perhaps it would be wise instead to work toward an understanding of the phenomenon and the individuals who commit this crime—to find ways to mitigate its impact while the odds are still in our favor.

1

Recognizing the Lethal Employee

No one can possibly know what is about to happen: it is happening, each time, for the first time, for the only time.

—James Baldwin
The Price of the Ticket

The emergence of the lethal employee is a relatively new, and deeply disturbing, phenomenon in America. This murderer, who is almost always male, represents an unforeseen threat to the American workplace, which cannot yet be accurately quantified or completely understood. He is causing an unexpected reevaluation of the meaning of the American workplace because his actions have redefined the risks of earning a living in this country. The idyllic concept of limitless opportunity provided by the American business community has, for many generations, been a consistent national tradition. Inherent in this view of the workplace is the expectation of safety and security for the majority of professions. The emerging possibility of being murdered at work is generally unthinkable and painfully antithetical to this traditional view of the workplace. Even when recognized, the possibility of being murdered at work is dismissed as statistically insignificant or unlikely to affect a particular work environment. Such an attitude, although understandable, is a dangerous act of denial, which can, and does, exacerbate the impact of workplace homicide by ignoring the real possibility of recognizing a potentially lethal situation before it has fully developed. The attitude of denial is often a source of organizational paralysis when prevention and intervention should be the first order of business. Disregarding the impact of occupational homicide because it is perceived as distant or unlikely sets the stage for future violence and murder much closer to home.

Since the mid-1980s many Americans have become aware of the possibilities of occupational homicide because, sadly, an unacceptable number of citizens have become victims of this crime. Press and television reports about occupational homicide have appeared with increasing frequency since 1986, and it is now rare that the American workweek is not closed out with one or more incidents of murder in the workplace. This new trend of murdering American workers has become a possibility with which every working man and woman must cope. Unfortunately, for vast numbers of American workers, this crime is perceived as a remote, impersonal event. It should be obvious, however, that it is not. This is a crime that, in many ways, has become a new workplace tradition—and it can potentially affect any worker in any organization.

Many incidents of occupational homicide are, in fact, crimes of mass murder. Multiple employees are regularly slain in acts of revenge by current or ex-employees whose ultimate aggression strikes at the work environment. In many instances, such killings have a random quality and are seemingly without purpose or sense; the victims may have no significant relationship with the murderer, or their relationship may have been that of familiar and trusted coworkers. In other incidents, employees are slaughtered because of unfortunate circumstances that placed them in the path of a murderer intent on revenge against a specific coworker. Increasingly, supervisors are targeted for their actions, which they may have felt were beneficial to the organization and its employees. Workers in government agencies are not only killed by frustrated clients who have tired of the bureaucracy into which they have been thrust, they are also targeted by angry and frustrated coworkers because they were unable to cope with an impersonal, deteriorating working environment or did not receive appropriate intervention when it was desperately needed. A spurned lover may target the individual with whom he is obsessed, but he is just as likely to commit multiple murders in an effort to carry out his act of revenge. A fired ex-employee may return to the organization and kill randomly, taking his revenge without regard to who becomes his next victim by enacting a symbolic crime designed to obliterate the entire company. The possibilities of an employee being caught in the crossfire of an individual intent on the ultimate crime in the workplace are growing and, without effective intervention, they may become limitless.

Why, in the past decade, has the American workplace become a modern arena for violence by members of its own workforce? Who are the employee-perpetrators, and why do they so devalue life as to take it indiscriminately and, frequently, without apparent remorse? What can be done to reverse this trend of mayhem against the American business community before the definition of the workplace as a haven of opportunity is transformed into one in which an employee risks his or her life solely for the purposes of pursuing a career?

These are not idle questions, and they do not lend themselves to simple answers. The motivations of a workplace murderer are complex; the crime is not always a simple one with a clear and precise meaning. This is especially true when the murderer is an employee or ex-employee; when homicide takes place, not in the commission of another crime, but for reasons that are convoluted, perhaps pathological, and directly related to the work environment. The impact of this crime, because it is so often committed by an employee of the organization, is enormous both in terms of lives needlessly lost and of organizational disruption. In effect, the crime of occupational homicide perpetrated by an employee holds the American business community hostage from within, in an ominous and unpredictable manner—in a way that must ultimately be overcome by those same individuals who are most likely to become its victims. The American worker, in the final analysis, must be prepared for the eventuality of a murderous coworker and have in hand the skills and methods to ensure prevention. The employee or supervisor who desires to remain safe at work must be capable of reasonably identifying all risks to his or her life, including the risk presented by a potentially lethal coworker.

VIOLENCE AND MURDER IN THE WORKPLACE

In August 1993, the National Institute for Occupational Safety and Health (NIOSH, U.S. Department of Health and Human Services) published the results of a long-term study on fatal injuries to American workers. This was the first major longitudinal study undertaken by the federal government to examine the causes of death in the workplace, and it remains to this day a primary source of information about workplace homicide. The NIOSH study covered the decade 1980-1989 and provided information about all manner of employee deaths in the workplace. A disturbing revelation of this research was that homicide was a significant contributor to the death rate of American workers—much more significant than would have been thought possible a decade before the publication of the NIOSH data. According to this research, 63,589 workers died from injuries on the job during the decade of the 1980s, with 14 percent of these deaths attributable to homicide—which was also the third leading cause of worker fatalities nationally. Even more disturbing was the fact that the leading cause of death for women in the workplace was homicide, accounting for 41 percent of all female worker fatalities.[1] Unsettling as these statistics were at the time of their publication, the danger they implied for the future was even greater.

A troublesome constraint of the research methodology used by NIOSH was the collection of data by way of traditional death certificate information reported from across the country. With a multitude of reporting sources, and a general uncertainty about how to report a workplace homicide, NIOSH determined that the number of workplace fatalities may have been underreported by as much as 33 percent and estimated that a minimum of 10 percent of such deaths were probably not recorded at all. NIOSH has made efforts to improve the methodology of gathering death certificate information since 1992, and future reports can be expected to more precisely convey the extent of workplace fatalities. Nonetheless, for the decade 1980-1989, it must be remembered that the number of workers killed at work (for any reason) may be significantly understated. This underreporting would also apply to the number of workplace homicide victims.

NIOSH used eleven occupational categorizations in its 1993 report to demonstrate the impact of worker death within easily defined career divisions. When viewed in this way, NIOSH identified workplace homicide as a leading cause of death in six of the eleven occupational categories, despite the fact that vital information on homicide from the states of New York, Oklahoma, Louisiana, and Nebraska was unavailable. Had complete data been available at the time of the NIOSH report, it is possible that homicide would have been a primary cause of worker death in even more occupational categories than initially reported. Occupations classified as Executive, Administrative or Managerial; Professional or Specialist; Transportation, Clerical, Service; and Sales all indicated occupational homicide as a leading cause of worker death. In some classifications, such as Executive, Administrative or Managerial; Sales and Service, workplace homicide significantly predominated all other reasons for worker death.

When examined by geographical location, homicide was either the foremost or secondary cause of workplace fatalities in thirteen states and Washington, D.C. In the nation's capitol, homicide was the *leading* cause of worker death, as it was in the states of Connecticut, Michigan, and South Carolina. In several populous states, such as California, Florida, Illinois, and New Jersey, homicide was the *second leading* cause of death in the workplace.[2]

Of all homicide victims identified during the survey period, 80 percent were male. Even though homicide was the leading cause of death for female workers, a male in the workplace was three times more likely to become a victim of homicide than a female (because of the male-predominated demography of the workplace in the decade studied). A worker in the age range of 25-44 years was more likely to be murdered at work than an employee in any other age group. Most victims of occupational homicide were slain with a firearm (80%). When ethnicity was considered, the homicide victim was most often white (75%), followed by blacks (19%), and other races (6%). At least 7,600 workers—an average of over 750 each year—were the victims of homicide during the decade under study. As stated in the NIOSH report, this number is believed to be conservative.

As the decade of the 1990s began, the impact of occupational homicide on the American workforce became even more significant. By 1992, the annual number of workplace homicide victims exceeded 1,000, and by the next year there were clear indications that this category of crime was continuing to increase at an alarming rate. For example, in that year, the state of California identified occupational homicide as the *leading* cause of death to workers, surpassing even the death count attributable to traffic accidents.[i] By 1994, it was estimated that workplace homicide was the cause of 17 percent of all worker fatalities, continuing the trend of annual increases that was first noticed in the original NIOSH research data.[3]

Disregarding such heinous acts of terrorism as the bombing of the federal building in Oklahoma City on April 19, 1995 (in which 169 persons were killed), the rate of occupational homicide continues to increase each year and, in some areas of the country, at a serious pace. Significantly, these alarming statistics do not account for the additional one million workers who are the victims of some form of workplace violence each year—violence that can sometimes lead to murder.[4] There can be little doubt that workplace violence in all forms, including occupational homicide, has reached troublesome proportions in the United States.

Since the release of the NIOSH data covering the decade 1980-1989, several other studies have been undertaken in an effort to more precisely define the crime of occupational homicide and come to an understanding of the actions and motivations of the perpetrator. In 1995, the Law Enforcement Bulletin (published by the U.S. Department of Justice and the Federal Bureau of Investigation) carried an article (contributed by T. Stanley Duncan) dealing with incidents of significant violence in the workplace.[5] The research included a review of 89 incidents that occurred between May, 1988 and May, 1994, each of which involved a major occurrence of workplace violence (including homicide). This study revealed useful statistical information about the characteristics of workplace murderers and their victims:

1. While the average age of perpetrators of non-workplace murders in America was typically under 30 years during the survey period (and remains so today), the average age of workplace murderers in this study was 38.2 years. Only two of the perpetrators were under 25 years of age.
2. Of all workplace murderers, 97 percent were male.
3. In every incident, a firearm was used to commit the crime.
4. Of the perpetrators, 41 percent were current employees at the time they committed their crime, while 46 percent were former employees. The remaining 13 percent of the perpetrators were either domestic partners of an employee or clients of the victimized organization.
5. Of the organizations victimized by occupational homicide, 38 percent were governmental agencies of some type, most often federally related, with the U.S. Postal Service the most frequently victimized employer. This figure represented a disproportionately large percentage of all organizations victimized by workplace violence in that only 15 percent of the American workforce was employed by these agencies during the survey period.
6. The average number of fatalities for each incident was 2.5, with at least one individual murdered in 39 percent of the cases. This means that in well over one third of the incidents surveyed at least one employee was slain.

---

i. In that year, 195 Californians were murdered at work while 125 died in traffic accidents.

The profile of the perpetrator of workplace homicide implied by this data is of a male employee or ex-employee, at or approaching middle age, who is familiar and comfortable with firearms, intent on revenge, lethal in his intentions, and quite capable of murdering several individuals in the short course of his crime. As will be evident throughout the case histories in this book, such a profile is overwhelmingly common for a workplace murderer. In addition, the perpetrator will sometimes kill randomly, perhaps ending such a siege by taking his own life at the murder scene or somewhere in the proximity of the crime site. A recent, and more disturbing, trend is that the murderer may use a military-style assault weapon during his rampage in order to inflict maximum damage upon his victims. In an increasing number of incidents, multiple weapons are brought to the scene by the perpetrator, further indicating his clear intention to maximize the ensuing violence. This perpetrator will often start his rampage by targeting a supervisor or ex-supervisor against whom he holds a grudge. In fact, recent Federal Bureau of Investigation (FBI) data suggests that incidents of this particular form of workplace homicide—employee against supervisor—have more than doubled in the past ten years. This increase does not include incidents in which an employee killed a coworker or in which the employee returned to the organization for retribution after his employment had been terminated.[6]

This is only a preliminary outline of the worker who is hell-bent on revenge at any cost. There are other characteristics that can be identified and will prove useful in more accurately profiling the potentially lethal employee. However, all lethal workers share at least one characteristic—once he has made the decision to kill, he will be well prepared for whatever is to come, often disregarding loss of life to others or himself. Once committed, it is unlikely he will be deterred until his revenge has been satisfied, his rampage has been stopped by force, or he has taken his own life in a final act of aggression. The challenge, then, for all workplace personnel is to understand enough about the lethal employee to prevent his actions or, failing that, to minimize the mayhem and death that will inevitably result from his attack.

The Employee as Murderer

Occupational homicide is often an act perpetrated during the commission of another crime, such as armed robbery. This is an unfortunate, but pervasive, scenario in certain industries such as the retail trades. However, many workplace homicides are committed by current employees or employees who have recently left an organization, to which they then return to act out their crime. In many such cases, the perpetrator is more deadly in terms of victims than his counterpart who murders during the commission of another crime. It is not uncommon for such a perpetrator to murder at least two individuals, and often, many more. In short, he may sometimes resort to mass murder in seeking his revenge. Of even greater significance is the growing body of evidence indicating that the lethal employee will sometimes kill indiscriminately, thereafter ending his murder rampage by an act of suicide. The lethal employee is able to attack the workplace easily because he is known to coworkers and supervisors; he usually has access to the work site and is not typically regarded as a potential murderer. This advantage makes him a particularly significant threat to the work environment.

In order to add structure to any attempt to understand the actions of a lethal employee, it is necessary to construct a precise definition of the term *employee* in relation to the crime of occupational homicide. This may, at first, seem obvious and simple; but it is not. Employees do not become lethal within understood guidelines, timetables, or other parameters. There are many incidents in the literature in which a current employee commits murder in the workplace, but these acts are almost always unexpected. There are also many such crimes committed by employees who have been fired from their jobs or who have left the organization for other reasons but return to seek revenge; once again, retribution in the form of murder is rarely anticipated by coworkers or supervisors. There is simply no way of knowing when a potentially violent employee will react in a lethal manner. In view of the increasing incidents of terminated employees who return to victimize an organization, and given the unpredictable nature of the crime itself, it makes sense to consider the lethal employee as one who is *currently employed at the target organization or was in its employ within the year prior to an act of occupational homicide.* This is, admittedly, an artificial structure, but it should account for such motivational factors as firing for cause, downsizing, and layoffs—all actions that have become increasingly common in the current economic climate of the American business community.

There is precious little hard data available about the lethal employee and his actions in the workplace. The majority of information about this crime, and about the perpetrator, is only available in the media—which is not always a source of accurate information and often lacks sufficient detail. Still, the potential effects of the lethal employee are becoming well known to many Americans because the actions of the perpetrator are so often grievous and highly publicized. An assumption can be made that many Americans are somewhat familiar with the potential impact of workplace homicide yet lack sufficient understanding of motivation, intervention, and protection.

The murders committed by the lethal employee are particularly disturbing because they are carried out by a single individual, often known to his victims, who is not typically regarded as a potential murderer. In many instances, this particular crime—one committed by a known coworker—is significantly compounded by acts of denial in the workplace, which may cause employees or supervisors to ignore or dismiss overt indications of potential violence. In many incidents of workplace murder, the intentions of the lethal employee are telegraphed long before he commits to violence. Often, these intentions, which are expressed in the form of behavioral warning signs, are not recognized and acted on quickly enough to protect the work environment. The concept of a worker murdering other workers known to him is, after all, not one that can be embraced comfortably by members of the workforce; the crime is compounded and aided in its effect because it is often not conceivable, even to potential victims. Statistics make clear, however, that this *is* a major category of crime (which is increasing, with an obvious escalation in lethal results), which is perpetrated by a criminal often known to his victims but rarely recognized for his violent potential.

PROFILE OF THE LETHAL EMPLOYEE

Profiling the potentially lethal employee is an exercise in both art and science. There is no question that many potential workplace murderers will not match any predefined profile. Nonetheless, there are patterns evident in the behavior of workplace murderers that make the effort of profiling them worthwhile and important to any organizational prevention program. The lethal employee often telegraphs his violent intentions well before acting upon them; he will frequently behave in a manner that is at least somewhat predictable, and which itself may predict violence. An understanding of the personal and behavioral characteristics most frequently associated with an individual likely to commit violence in the workplace can provide the basis for intervention, staff training, and deterrence. This knowledge, when used carefully and with understanding, can provide some advantage to a workforce that would otherwise be unprepared for possible violence. However, despite this advantage, such an analysis can never be perfect because it attempts to predict the intentions and actions of another human being—an endeavor that is difficult, at best. Profiling the potentially lethal employee is an exercise in art and science that offers some prevention possibilities—it is not a guarantee of safety.

Knowledge of occupational homicide and the potentially lethal employee has increased considerably since the issue was first recognized by the public in 1986.[ii] This knowledge has been derived from a growing number of actual workplace homicides and, therefore, lends a somewhat reliable history to the issue. However, despite this history, there is still much to be learned in terms of recognizing the potentially lethal employee and implementing more effective safety and security programs in American organizations. The developing understanding of who may become a workplace murderer provides a reason for optimism about an issue that is inherently disturbing; but this compendium of knowledge is not great. The ability to identify the developing signs of aggression that may lead to homicide in the workplace is crucial to reversing the decade-long trend of increasing wrongful death among the American workforce; however, this ability is not foolproof. The growing knowledge of the history of this crime, although painful, represents a potential weapon of defense for any work environment; nonetheless, it is still only a *potential* defense

---

ii. This was the year of the Edmond Post Office massacre—a case history in this book.

strategy. The emerging issue of workplace homicide will not succumb easily to understanding or prevention; however, a knowledge of the history of this crime, combined with an understanding of the behavior and motives of the perpetrator, may provide the starting point for more effective methods of protecting the work environment.

Given what is known about the behavior and characteristics of workplace murderers, it is possible to construct a working profile that may be of use in the process of identifying the potentially lethal employee. Although it is certainly not a perfect instrument of prediction, such a profile can be applied with reasonable accuracy to the majority of known workplace murderers. There is, therefore, reason to believe that, if properly understood and utilized, it can be helpful in predicting potential violence.

The profile that follows was developed through extensive research into many cases of occupational homicide. In this sense, it is known to have historical validity. Hopefully, this historical reliability will enhance its use as a predictive tool for similar, future situations. Within the structure of the profile, certain characteristics have been given a probability to denote their frequency when considering the actions of a potentially violent individual. These probabilities have also been derived from the history of occupational homicide in this country and, in this sense, can be considered historically reliable. Whether they will prove accurate in predicting future incidents of workplace violence must remain an open issue. There will, unfortunately, always be exceptions to any profile.

The profile itself has been constructed to reflect two major categories considered useful in the prediction of violence—personal characteristics and behavioral characteristics. *Personal characteristics* attempt to define sex, age, and life-experience characteristics that are common to workplace murderers. *Behavioral characteristics* can generally be considered as independent of the sex, age, or life experiences of the potentially lethal individual. A combination of these elements, personal and behavioral, helps to more precisely define the potentially lethal employee.

Personal Characteristics of the Potentially Lethal Employee

The potentially lethal employee will most likely be male. Various survey results set this probability as low as 80 percent and as high as 97 percent. Much of the uncertainty in this range is due to the lack of a comprehensive database of incidents of occupational homicide. The crime is most frequently reported in the mass media which often omits pertinent and reliable information. However, the personal characteristics of workplace murderers (such as age and sex) are typically reported in the press and are generally reliable if more than a single source of information is obtained. A review of many incidents of murder in the workplace indicated that the overwhelming majority of perpetrators were male. A conservative estimate of this probability would be 80 percent, although the actual preponderance of male perpetrators is likely greater, with a more realistic probability of 95 percent.

The ethnicity of the potentially lethal employee will most likely be white. This is a historical characteristic that, in recent years, may be undergoing a change with the shifting demographics of the American workplace. As efforts to diversify the workplace become more effective over time, it is possible that this characteristic may become less reliable. Historically, the lethal employee has typically been a middle-class, working, white male. In 1996, this characteristic remains fundamentally reliable because (1) the working middle class in America remains generally dominated by white males, and (2) women rarely commit workplace homicide. There is no reason to assume, however, that this indicator will remain static. There is inherently no basis to assert that white males constitute the majority of workplace murderers for reasons other than (1) their predominance in certain areas of the workforce, and (2) the fact they are demonstrably more aggressive than their female counterparts in virtually all aspects of society. For these reasons, the personal characteristic of ethnicity is given a provisional probability of 70 percent with the caveat that it cannot be considered wholly reliable and will most probably indicate a decrease in reliability over time.

The age of the potentially lethal employee will most likely be over thirty and less than sixty years. A review of many case histories of workplace homicide demonstrates clearly that the lethal employee is typically over the age of thirty and is often in his forties or early fifties. It is rare that an employee over the age of sixty is the perpetrator in an incident of workplace murder. Similarly, it is unusual, although not without exception, for an employee to commit murder while under the age of thirty. The case histories in this book demonstrate the most typical ages at which an employee commits murder in the workplace—significantly favoring the thirty-to-sixty age range.[iii] The probability attributed to this characteristic is 75 percent. This probability should be considered provisional for at least one disturbing reason—the typical age of the lethal employee appears to be decreasing when incidents of workplace homicide are examined only over the most recent two-year period. This could be a statistical aberration, since any analysis of incidents of workplace homicide is made difficult by a lack of accessible information about the perpetrator; however, it may also indicate the emergence of a new trend. It is not possible to draw meaningful conclusions at this time. This is a characteristic that mandates careful and continuing observation in the event that workplace murderers may, in the future, not comport with the generally accepted age category of thirty to sixty years.

The potentially lethal employee may be socially isolated. In many incidents of workplace homicide, the perpetrator has been found to be unusually isolated socially. Perhaps he lived alone for many years, recently changed job

---

iii. Possible reasons for this relatively predictable characteristic of the lethal employee are examined in Chapter 3.

locations, or suffered a separation or divorce. It is also possible that the individual did not live completely alone but was psychologically isolated from those with whom he lived and thus unable to benefit from strong social links domestically. Whatever the reason, when social isolation is apparent in the lifestyle of an individual, there may be an increased propensity for violence—given, of course, other behavioral and circumstantial considerations. Many incidents of workplace homicide have been committed by men who were clearly and significantly alone in a psychological, or even physical, sense. Often the job itself was a crucial form of socialization for the perpetrator. Once that job was gone, for whatever reason, the individual became dangerously isolated and, over time, resorted to violence. The connection between social isolation and violence appears strong but has not been satisfactorily demonstrated statistically. Nonetheless, an argument can easily be made that many workplace murderers clearly exhibit this characteristic—numerous actual incidents make this self-evident. Therefore, this characteristic has been given a provisional probability of 50 percent to indicate its importance as a potential contributor to violence.

The potentially lethal employee will have experienced one or more triggering events prior to acting out violently, at least one of which will be directly linked to his violent actions. A *triggering event* can be defined as an incident, regardless of how minor, that induces the potentially violent individual to commit to a course of violence. It is the proverbial "straw that broke the camel's back" and, like that straw, may often be perceived by others with far less significance than it is perceived by the perpetrator. Frustration, a sense of helplessness or abandonment, and a sense of loss of control frequently contribute to a continuum of experiences that chip away at an individual's ability to cope with even minor stressors. This pattern of failure and frustration, culminating in physical violence, is a common theme in the lives of workplace murderers, who may have fantasized about violent retribution for some time. Once they have reached such a high-pitched, dangerous level of frustration, it may only take a minor incident to activate their latent intentions to become violent. In these situations it may be difficult to pinpoint a specific triggering event but it is usually possible to identify a series of such incidents that can be considered contributors to violence. In other circumstances, such as when an individual is fired or laid off from his job, the triggering event will be more obvious. Other major life stressors, such as the death of a loved one or the dissolution of an important personal relationship, should also be viewed as possible triggering events for the potentially lethal employee. There are, in fact, limitless possibilities for an incident to prove to be a triggering event in the life of an individual who is driven toward violence. This characteristic has been attributed a probability range of 75 percent to 90 percent, although the lower extent is probably conservative. It is possible that virtually all incidents of workplace homicide bear a direct relationship to some triggering event (as experienced by the perpetrator). The uncertainty of the assigned probability range expresses the frequent inability to precisely identify such a triggering event after the crime has been committed because it was not obvious or the perpetrator died without identifying it.

Behavioral Characteristics of the Potentially Lethal Employee

The potentially lethal employee will exhibit one or more key behavioral warning signs that are considered to be general predictors of violence. These behavioral warning signs do not predict future violence to a certainty, but one or more are nearly always present in an individual who ultimately commits a violent act, particularly homicide. The characteristics used in this profile have been derived from the behavioral sciences and were presented in their original form by authors S. A. Baron and E. D. Wheeler in their book, *Violence in Our Schools, Hospitals and Public Places.*[7] As more has been learned about the behavior and motivations of the lethal employee, it has been possible to refine and more precisely apply these characteristics to actual incidents of occupational homicide and general workplace violence. These ten behavioral warning signs have stood the tests of time and research; today, as when they were first presented by Baron and Wheeler, these characteristics provide an effective methodology of predicting future violence from the viewpoint of current behavior. So pervasive are these characteristics that they have been assigned strong probabilities of being evident in the potentially lethal employee:

1. A 90 percent probability that the individual will exhibit at least one behavioral warning sign.
2. A 50 percent probability that the individual will exhibit two or more behavioral warning signs.

Without question, it is difficult to assess the probabilities of violence implied by certain behavioral warning signs. The knowledge and reporting of incidents of occupational homicide rarely provide sufficient information about the perpetrator to develop a strong database of characteristics from which reliable statistics can be derived. However, a review of many incidents of occupational homicide does indicate that some behavioral warning signs seem to be in evidence more frequently than others. It is therefore reasonable to assume that certain behavior will carry more weight in any attempt to assess the probabilities of future violence. For this reason, and as a preliminary working model, it is reasonable to assign relative degrees of frequency to each behavioral characteristic, based on what is known about actual incidents of workplace homicide. Clearly, this is not a very precise methodology, and in the final analysis, it may prove impossible to favor some behavioral warning signs over others. Nonetheless, actual incidents do seem to indicate a relative preponderance of certain behavioral patterns. Therefore, each of the behavioral warning signs will be assigned a relative frequency of *common*, *neutral* (or *unknown*), or *uncommon* based upon what has been learned from incidents of occupational homicide found in the literature. Clearly, these assignments must not be considered infallible; they may change over time as more is learned about the complex issues surrounding murder in the workplace. At best, they provide an informal guide to what has been learned over the last decade about this crime and the behavioral characteristics most often associated with its commission:

A history of violent behavior (frequency common). This is perhaps the most reliable indicator of potential violence. An individual who demonstrates a history, or pattern, of violent behavior will be prone to repeat that behavior in the future. It is important to avoid defining prior violent behavior too narrowly when considering this characteristic as a predictor of future violence. Violent behavior embodies a continuum of activities that range from the vocalization of violence to homicide or suicide. Along this range of behavior there are many variations in how violence may be expressed or exhibited. Certainly, a history of threatening behavior, whether vocalized or not, can be considered a precursor to physical violence, even in the absence of evidence of prior significant physical violence. Although the argument can be made that historical evidence of violence is not a guaranty of future violent behavior, an understanding of any form of violent criminal activity clearly supports the contention that a history of violence is often a predictor of future violence. An individual who elects to resolve problems or obtain satisfaction in a violent manner is unlikely to alter this behavior in the near term without professional and effective intervention. For this reason, and based upon significant historical evidence of the relationship between past and future violent behavior, this is considered a primary behavioral warning sign which should never be ignored or given anything but serious consideration.

Evidence of psychosis or a similar severe psychological disorder (frequency unknown). Psychosis can be defined as a *loss of contact with reality* or *loss of the ability to process experience appropriately.*[8] This general condition can embrace more specific psychological disorders such as schizophrenia, schizophreniform or schizoaffective disorders, psychotic episodes, substance-induced psychotic disorders, and a variety of delusional disorders.[9] A psychotic individual is, by definition, one who has great difficulty coping with the ordinary responsibilities of life and who may, under certain conditions, become violent to him or herself or others. A psychosis may be transitory and last for only a few hours or days, or it can last for many months or years. Because there are a variety of disorders linked with a psychotic state, it is difficult for the layperson to distinguish among the many clinical possibilities. In the context of developing possibilities for violence prevention, however, a fine distinction among possible psychotic states is not necessary. It is sufficient to be able to recognize the presence of a psychosis and, from an evaluation of the exhibited behavior, determine if there is at least a potential for violence. In general, psychotic individuals can, and sometimes do, react unpredictably and violently. Because they are not capable of consistently processing their experiences in an appropriate manner and, in fact, may often experience a very different reality than those in their proximity, an individual suffering from any disorder accompanied by a psychotic state presents the potential for a sudden and unexpected violent reaction. An individual suffering from a psychosis should receive prompt and professional intervention. Because the psychotic state is inherently unpredictable, an individual so afflicted should not be given amateur attention or made the target of unwarranted intrusion. This behavioral warning sign is best diagnosed by a professional in the behavioral sciences, and any resultant intervention should be undertaken at a similarly professional level (see Table 1.1).

Table 1.1: General Indicators of a Psychosis

Delusions or hallucinations that are typically bizarre and may be auditory
Inability to function effectively in a social or occupational setting
Disorganized or incoherent behavior or speech
Significant paranoia accompanied by delusional thinking
Unusual physical activity or motor activity
Extreme negativism or fear
Incoherent and inappropriate communications with others
Disorganized or incoherent thought process

Obsession with another individual, romance obsession, or a severe delusional disorder that results in behavior targeting another individual, such as stalking (frequency neutral in cases of multiple homicide, common in cases of homicide committed against a single individual). There are a number of variations of this behavior, which range from clinical to practical in terms of recognition. From a clinical perspective, this behavior is considered a subtype of a *delusional disorder* defined as *erotomania*. In this form, the behavior involves a predominate delusional theme that another person is in love with the affected individual. This delusion leads to behavior that is often referred to as *stalking* and involves activities such as sending numerous letters, making persistent telephone calls, conducting surveillance, sending gifts, making frequent visits, and using similar tactics of harassment.[10] Individuals suffering from this disorder may eventually be provoked to violence when the rejection of their advances becomes intolerable. They may also commit violence against others in an attempt to impress the person who is the object of their obsession.

A more practical method of interpreting and understanding this kind of behavior was offered by Park E. Dietz, M.D., Ph.D., and involves the definition of three subtypes of the romantic stalker: (1) the spurned ex-lover or spouse who is acting out a motivation of revenge, (2) the individual suffering from an obvious delusional disorder, and (3) the individual suffering from a pathological dependence upon another person who becomes obsessed with him or her.[11] An individual suffering from this disorder, regardless of classification, can become violent if he or she is sufficiently frustrated, psychotic, or unable to satisfactorily resolve the untenable relationship. Of particular concern is the ex-lover or spouse whose revenge can result in workplace violence (known as *spillover* violence) or the individual suffering from a pathological dependence upon a coworker. These individuals will sometimes act out their aggressions in the work environment with little or no regard for the effects of their behavior on innocent individuals. There are a surprising number of incidents of multiple homicide (two or more individuals murdered) in the workplace that can be attributed to an obsessive or delusional relationship with a coworker, lover or spouse. Cases of spillover violence have also increased in recent years and are frequently reported in the media.

Alcohol or chemical dependence (frequency unknown, but thought to be common). Most Americans are aware that the incidence of alcohol and chemical dependence in the United States is of epidemic proportions. Many organizations have provided employee assistance programs that offer sophisticated modalities of treatment for employees who are suffering from an addiction to one or more of these substances. However, the majority of individuals suffering such an addiction tend to not only deny their disability but also discount the catastrophic effects that can result from dependence upon alcohol or drugs. Of particular concern is the fact that the effect of some of these substances can result in violent or aggressive behavior (see Table 1.2). Substances such as phencyclidine (PCP), stimulants (amphetamines), and alcohol can induce extremely violent and unpredictable behavior. Even sedatives (tranquilizers), the most commonly abused substance in America other than alcohol, can lead to violent behavior through the cycle of dependence, withdrawal, and reassertion of the need for the drug. In addition, some prescription medications can induce violent behavior that is completely unforeseen in certain individuals. The extent to which substance abuse contributes to murder in the workplace is unknown to a certainty because such data is not available. However, given the pervasive problem of substance abuse in America, it can be safely assumed that this disorder plays a significant role in many cases of occupational homicide. The effects of alcohol and drugs are sufficiently understood that evidence of substance abuse by an employee, particularly in combination with other behavioral warning signs, must be considered a significant predictor of potential violence.

Severe or chronic depression (frequency common to the extent that some indicators of depression are evident in many incidents of workplace homicide). Depression is considered by many behavioral scientists to be the most pervasive psychological disorder in the United States. Estimates vary significantly on the numbers of Americans stricken by some form of depression each year, but many citations put this number at between 15 and 30 percent of the population. Despite its impact upon so many, this disorder is often dismissed entirely or not given adequate consideration in many American organizations or violence prevention programs.

Table 1.2: Commonly Abused Chemical Substances and Their Effects

Alcohol	A depressant associated with sedate behavior in some individuals and violently aggressive behavior in others. Potentially lethal when combined with certain drugs.
Marijuana	Increases heart rate, impairs short-term memory, impairs concentration, and induces feelings of euphoria. May induce anxiety, which can lead to violent behavior.
Hallucinogens (psychedelics)	Alters perception, induces illusions or hallucinations. Can lead to tremors, anxiety, recurrent memories, violent behavior, and organic brain damage.
Phencyclidine (PCP)	Induces extremely violent and aggressive behavior in many abusers. Frequently associated with uncontrollably aggressive behavior and self-injury.
Stimulants (amphetamines)	Potentially lethal effect even in small amounts. Frequent use leads to brain damage and death. Often associated with violent and aggressive behavior.
Sedatives (tranquilizers)	Depresses the central nervous system. Can be lethal when taken in conjunction with alcohol. Leads to dependence and aggressive behavior on withdrawal.
Narcotics (heroin, codeine)	Can be lethal with prolonged or increased use. Impairs reason and reactions. Leads to aggressive behavior on withdrawal or when used in certain forms.

Numerous individuals suffering from chronic depression will experience a *major depressive episode,* which can develop in a few days or weeks and last for up to six months or longer if untreated. During this episodic period, individuals may present a significant danger to themselves or others. Should an individual suffer a major depressive episode there is an increased possibility of suicide or other significantly violent behavior. The risk of violence is especially great if the episode is accompanied by psychotic features or the individual has a history of attempted suicide or other forms of violence. To add to the complexity of this disorder, virtually anyone can suffer such an episode following a significant psychosocial stressor such as the death of a loved one, divorce, separation, or loss of employment.[12] Thus, large numbers of American workers are potential victims of this disorder; a few of these individuals will react violently, while others may attempt to end their own lives. It is often difficult to assemble detailed information about the background or psychological condition of an employee who commits violence or murder in the workplace. Nonetheless, from those cases in which information was available, it can be demonstrated that the common indicators of depression, or a major depressive episode, were often in evidence (see Table 1.3). From the behavioral sciences it is known that depression increases the possibilities of violence, much of which is generally self-directed. Such violence can, however, be directed at others or carried out in a random way. Although there are varying statistics that address the issue of linking the symptoms of a major depressive episode with violent behavior, the most frequent citations put the probability between 7 and 15 percent for an individual acting out violently at some point in the course of the disorder. Even a most conservative estimate (say, 5 percent), given the huge number of Americans who suffer from depression in one form or another each year, results in a vast cadre of potentially violent employees. Clearly, very few individuals who react violently in the course of such an episode commit murder; in fact, such violence is typically self-directed. Nonetheless, there are many incidents of occupational homicide in the literature that make a clear connection between a major depressive episode and multiple murders in the workplace such that this disorder must be considered a significant predictor of potential violence.

Table 1.3: Indicators of a Major Depressive Episode[13]

Feelings of sadness, emptiness or worthlessness
Diminished interest in normal activities
Significant change in weight and/or appetite
Insomnia or hypersomnia
Psychomotor agitation or retardation
Reduction in normal levels of efficiency
Fatigue or loss of energy
Inappropriate feelings of guilt
Sorrowful, tearful appearance
Deterioration of physical appearance
Increased irritability and frustration
Reduced ability to concentrate and/or indecisiveness
Recurrent thoughts of death or suicide

Pathological blaming of others or the organization (frequency common). A pathological blamer will view other individuals, or an entire organization, as the fundamental cause of difficulties or obstacles that he is experiencing. Beyond blaming coworkers or the organization for his problems, the pathological blamer will frequently make threats of revenge regarding his plans to "get even" with those he perceives to be the cause of his difficulties. This type of blaming will usually be extreme, persistently vocalized, and far beyond what would be considered reasonable given the circumstances of the problem. The best test of whether the blaming is pathological is one of common sense. If an individual consistently blames coworkers or the organization for difficulties not related to their obvious relationship, and if this blaming is accompanied by threats (veiled or overt), the behavior should be considered pathological and a potential predictor of violence. This kind of blaming, if pervasive or pathological, can be considered as threatening even if actual threats are not vocalized.

Impaired neurological functioning (frequency uncommon). Although not commonly linked with occupational homicide, cases of *impaired neurological functioning* leading to murder can be found in the literature. This is an area of behavior that is difficult to recognize, even for professionals in the fields of medicine and the behavioral sciences. There have been cases recorded in which employees reacted with significant and sudden violence after exposure to certain chemicals or solvents which may have been absorbed through the skin or lungs. No doubt there are a variety of other cases that have not yet been recognized as attributable to physical elements in the work environment. This area of health science continues to receive the benefit of research from a variety of public agencies and private organizations in an effort to learn more about the effects of a range of chemical substances on the American worker. In relation to the prediction of violence, or its prevention, cases of impaired neurological functioning benefit most from the presence of a strong illness and injury prevention program within an organization whose employees are subjected to hazardous materials. The identification of behavioral warning signs attributable to this disorder makes the most sense in environments where the danger of exposure to chemical agents is high. Rigorous safety measures and routine physical screening can do much in terms of prevention in these environments. When assessing the potential for violence in such a workplace, the possibility of impaired neurological functioning must always be considered and should only be addressed by medical professionals.

Elevated frustration which is chronic or severe (frequency common). Employees face a variety of stressors in their lives and on the job. It is simply not possible for most workers to segregate the many challenges they face into clearly defined areas of concern and response. Domestic or financial problems cannot be left on the doorstep when an employee reports to the job site. Likewise, it is a virtual American tradition to bring challenges faced on the job into the home. Because of the continuum of challenges faced by American workers, the workplace is often the site of discussion and reaction to a wide variety of life stressors that may not be related to the work environment. Should an employee exhibit a sustained and significant level of frustration with personal issues, whether related to the work environment or not, there is the possibility of an eventual violent reaction. Success in employment and the workplace is an extremely important component of a meaningful and rewarding life. Relationships developed in the workplace can grow into long-term friendships or can deteriorate into violence. Likewise, relationships outside the work environment can have significant impact on the job. Regardless of the genesis of the frustration, the workplace is always at risk if an employee suffers unremitting and significant frustration for any reason. Often this frustration will be vocalized regularly by the affected employee, but it can also be exhibited by an unwillingness to cooperate with others, frequent arguments or disputes, the harassment of coworkers or clients, threatening behavior, theft, damage to property, statements of vengeance or revenge, and even attempts at suicide.

Chronic frustration and failure can be the genesis of mass murder, although the process that eventually results in homicide may be a prolonged one. It is not unusual to find that the lethal employee who suffers from chronic frustration commits multiple murders suddenly after having experienced a triggering event that pushes him beyond his ability to cope:

Typically the road to mass murder is long, lonely and rocky; it takes years before the perpetrator sees mass murder as the only way out. The mass slayer suffers a long history of frustration and failure, through childhood and on into his adult life. He has tremendous difficulty both at home and at work in achieving happiness and success. Over time, repeated frustration erodes his ability to cope so that even modest disappointments seem catastrophic.[14]

This behavioral warning sign is, therefore, one that can persist for years or decades before it erupts into physical violence. The prevention advantage associated with this warning sign is that it is generally quite obvious to coworkers when an employee is frustrated and angry for such a significant period of time; thus, there are usually significant opportunities for intervention. This is a classic behavioral warning sign that is persistent, typically apparent to others, and often associated with violence.

Weapons fetish, preoccupation with weaponry or paramilitary subjects, or a fascination with known cases of multiple workplace homicides (frequency common when a sustained interest in these subjects is in evidence). Nearly all workplace homicides are committed with a firearm. The most frequently used weapon is some type of handgun; however, in the past five years, various assault weapons have been used to commit murder in the workplace with increasing frequency and more deadly results. The workplace murderer is, therefore, typically able to acquire a firearm and generally knows how to use it. In fact, he is often an expert in the use of the weapons he possesses. One of the most common behavioral warning signs is frequently evidenced by an individual whose interest in weapons has become intense and who vocalizes this interest in a persistent manner. In many incidents of occupational homicide, the perpetrator talks about his knowledge and possession of weapons well before he commits to a violent act. This vocalization typically occurs in the work environment and is often directed to coworkers; it may take the form of veiled threats or it may be a conversational theme that tends to predominate his social interactions in the workplace. Although incidents of occupational homicide indicate that not all workplace murderers will speak about weaponry or paramilitary subjects prior to committing an act of violence, many will do so.

This is a particularly ominous indication if the conversation is predominated by themes of weapons, a weapons collection, or related paramilitary subjects in conjunction with publicized crimes of workplace shootings or murders. In addition to discussing weaponry or paramilitary subjects, the perpetrator may bring one or more of his firearms to the workplace and display them to coworkers or supervisors. Clearly, such activities must be interpreted as threatening to the workplace, even if no overt statements are made about the intended use of the weapons. Since firearms are, by far, the weapon of choice for workplace murderers, an individual who is demonstrating a preoccupation with these subjects or transporting them to the workplace must be considered as exhibiting a behavioral warning sign that should not be ignored.

A personality disorder that can result in violent or antisocial behavior (frequency unknown but possibly common for disorders such as antisocial personality disorder or borderline personality disorder). The personality of an individual is comprised of a set of behavioral patterns that remain generally consistent over time and by which he or she is defined and understood by others. When an individual suffers from a personality disorder, this consistency slips away and behavior may be perceived by others as bizarre, harmful, or violent. Of particular applicability to many perpetrators of occupational homicide are two personality disorders: *antisocial personality disorder* and *borderline personality disorder.* These crippling psychological disorders are often evident in individuals who resort to violence or murder in the workplace.

The term *sociopath* is commonly used to describe individuals suffering from *antisocial personality disorder.* The characteristics of an individual suffering from this disorder are typically those of significant hostility and aggression, a lack of concern for the safety of others, disregard for the effect of harmful actions, a lack of remorse for deeds that are harmful to others, and an extremely impulsive nature (see Table 1.4). These individuals are frequently unable to maintain a consistent level of performance at work and will often exhibit an erratic or poor work history. Recurring periods of unemployment and a pattern of frequently changing jobs may be prominent. These individuals are often involved in domestic violence and are likely to have some criminal background, even though it may be predominated by minor offenses. Individuals suffering from this disorder are unable to maintain a significant relationship with others and are prone to sudden and violent outbursts of anger. An interest in weapons, criminal activities, violence, and paramilitary issues is often associated with this disorder. An individual suffering from antisocial personality disorder is likely to commit acts of violence in the workplace and has a significant probability of committing murder if intervention is absent or not timely. This disorder is often associated with inferior socioeconomic conditions and urban settings. Antisocial personality disorder is significantly more prevalent in males than in females; it is also significantly apparent in many incidents of occupational homicide.[15]

Table 1.4: Indicators for Antisocial Personality Disorder

Disregard for the rights (or violation of the rights) of others
Repeated non-conformance to laws, regulations, and social norms
Deceitfulness and lying
Impulsive and erratic behavior
Irritability and aggressiveness
Reckless disregard for the safety and well-being of others
Consistent irresponsibility, both domestically and at work
Lack of remorse
Indifference to others

Individuals suffering from *borderline personality disorder*, as with individuals suffering from antisocial personality disorder, may pose a significant threat to the workplace even though they may not appear to be as overtly hostile or aggressive as the classic sociopath. Those suffering from borderline personality disorder will often be quite uncertain about many aspects of their lives and unable to make effective decisions about their future. They will act impulsively and, at times, in a threatening manner. Their moods will be unpredictable and punctuated by sudden outbursts of anger during which they may engage in physical fighting, the destruction of property, or other forms of violent behavior. When not aggressive, individuals suffering from this disorder may be quite charming and fully capable of manipulating others very successfully. Overall, the predominate theme inherent in the behavior associated with this disorder is one of instability (see Table 1.5). As contrasted with antisocial personality disorder, borderline personality disorder is diagnosed more frequently in females than in males.[16] Despite the diagnosis ratio of approximately four females to one male, this disorder can be identified in a number of workplace homicides committed by males.

In addition to the ten behavioral characteristics frequently evidenced by a potentially lethal employee, there are two additional behavioral warning signs, which are less technical in nature but are common precursors to physical violence. The value of these warning signs lies in their ease of understanding at all levels of an organization. Both can be considered important characteristics in the prediction of future violence:

The potentially lethal employee will vocalize, or otherwise act out, violent intentions prior to committing a violent act (frequency common). This behavioral characteristic should be considered extremely important. Violent behavior represents a continuum of activities that frequently escalate from the vocalization of aggression to physical violence. It is common for an individual who is contemplating violence in the workplace to vocalize this ideation, either overtly or as veiled threats. Unfortunately, it is a common practice in most work environments to dismiss this vocalization as just "blowing off steam." This can often be a fatal error in judgment. Any employee who is vocalizing thoughts of retaliation, vengeance, or violence in the work environment must be taken quite seriously. This is particularly true if the vocalization is persistent or a theme of violence is pervasive.

Table 1.5: Indicators for Borderline Personality Disorder

Significant fear of real or imagined abandonment
Pattern of unstable interpersonal relationships
Unstable sense of self or self-identity
Impulsive, self-damaging behavior
Suicidal behavior
Behavior threatening to self or others
Unstable moods and reactions
Chronic feelings of emptiness
Inappropriate and intense outbursts of anger
Fighting and other forms of physical aggression
Paranoid ideation or severe dissociative symptoms

Over a sustained period of time, the potentially lethal employee will exhibit behavior that is interpreted as strange, bizarre, threatening, or uncomfortable to multiple coworkers (frequency common). Often overlooked, even in comprehensive violence prevention programs, is the fact that employees tend to know the behavioral characteristics of their coworkers quite well and often quite accurately. That is, they are typically versed in the personalities of their coworkers and, therefore, often the first to perceive any significant change in behavior. Unfortunately, there are many cases of occupational homicide that indicate that coworkers were deeply concerned with the behavior of an individual in the work environment yet no intervention was pursued. It is a common practice for employees to share confidences and build a bond of trust in the workplace. In some situations, this ordinarily beneficial camaraderie can, in itself, compound a potentially violent situation by closing down lines of communication that could have otherwise provided an opportunity for intervention. Since coworkers are typically familiar with the personalities and behavior patterns of those around them in the workplace, an obvious prevention methodology would be to ensure that, when issues of safety are involved, the working environment benefits from free and open communication. It is equally important that employees and supervisors be sensitive to an individual whose behavior has changed significantly and who may be in need of immediate assistance. Even though very few employees commit murder in the workplace, other acts of violence are quite common. It is almost always the case that an employee will exhibit some form of behavior that indicates the potential for violence, even if this behavior is subtle and easily dismissed. The two essential factors in implementing a prevention program to address this aspect of workplace violence are (1) a staff that is trained to observe the early warning signs of an employee in difficulty, and (2) a methodology in place to intervene with the employee in a positive and confidential manner (see Table 1.6). If intervention is provided for an employee exhibiting early indications of distress, there is a significant reduction in the possibility of a violent outcome; however, this is only true if recognition is effective and appropriate action is undertaken at an early stage.

Table 1.6: Indicators for Immediate Employee Intervention

Avoidance of the workplace through unwarranted absences or tardiness
Extreme reliance on supervisor(s) or unwarranted need for supervision
Failing productivity by a previously productive employee
Deteriorating job performance by a previously good performer
Deteriorating or hostile workplace relationships and/or client relationships
Significant increase in incidents of errors, mistakes, or safety violations
Indications of stress or depression that are severe and sustained
Indications of alcohol and/or substance abuse
Persistent indications of other key behavioral warning signs (such as a preoccupation with weapons, violence, or violent incidents)

The Uncertainty of Prediction

Authors James Fox and Jack Levin, in their book, *Overkill: Mass Murder and Serial Killing Exposed*, offered an excellent observation about the attempt to profile a potentially lethal employee, particularly one who may resort to mass murder in the workplace:

Profiles designed to predict rare events, such as workplace mass murder, tend to overpredict, producing a large percentage of "false positives." Regardless of the specific profile characteristics, many more employees will likely fit the profile than will in fact seek revenge at work. There is a very large haystack of angry, frustrated employees who never smile and are always ready to blame others for their shortcomings and make threatening statements, but very few needles who will in fact commit mass murder.[17]

When evaluating any profiling scenario, these are wise words indeed. There are few truly lethal employees in the American workforce. However, those who do become lethal often commit multiple murders in what may appear to be an indiscriminate manner.

In an absolute sense, it is nearly impossible to predict when, or if, an employee will become lethal. Attempting to make such a prediction involves the analysis of complex modalities of behavior and an understanding of personal motivations, which often results in nothing more than educated guesswork. The basis for any ability to predict future violence relies completely on historical incidents, which, although numerous, are rarely reported with complete accuracy or full details. The most to be achieved is a recognition of the behavioral patterns that often precede occupational homicide and, derived from these, the assumption that such patterns will hold true for future incidents. Such a process embodies an obvious risk of error.

Most Americans are at least somewhat aware of the well-publicized successes and failures that arise from following opinions offered by professionals in the behavioral sciences. Incidents of a misdiagnosis in a criminal proceeding, parole hearing, or clinical environment are frequent. They are also understandable considering the uncertainties inherent in human behavior. Even more uncertain is any attempt to predict the future behavior of a *potentially* violent employee. Nonetheless, some effort must be made to provide an increased level of protection to the American workplace. Without question, the crime of occupational homicide continues to take an unprecedented and unnecessary toll in terms of human life and economic losses throughout the American business community, in both the public and private sectors. Since this crime cannot be assuaged after the fact, it is obvious that some effort must be made to predict, and therefore avoid, potential violence.

The efficacy of profiling a potentially lethal employee is slowly improving as more is learned about this heinous crime. Unfortunately, the effect of occupational homicide on most Americans is distant and easily dismissed. This is understandable from a certain point of view because the subject itself is unsettling. However, it cannot be ignored. Occupational homicide has become a significant threat to virtually any American organization and is therefore a possibility, even if remote, for most workers.

In attempting to profile the potentially lethal employee, two important points must be considered: (1) the effort is surely a combination of art and science, which is subject to error and misinterpretation, and (2) the profiling process is evolving rapidly and will be more reliable in the future than it is today. Therefore, although crucial to any effort to protect the work environment, the characteristics or behavioral warning signs used to predict violence must always be considered provisional, subject to change, and easily misinterpreted if not used correctly and by trained individuals (see Table 1.7).

Indicators for Intervention

Coworkers and supervisors are often the best source of violence prevention because they are usually the first to notice a significant change in behavior on the part of their colleagues. Since the path to violence is generally one of behavioral escalation, it is frequently possible to detect the early indications of a worker experiencing stressors or circumstances that may eventually result in a violent reaction. Although there are individuals who will react with sudden and unpredictable violence, this is exceptional. Instead, most employees who become violent or lethal exhibit an identifiable escalation in aggressive behavior that is apparent to coworkers and supervisors. This pattern of escalation provides an opportunity for intervention that is crucial to protecting the work environment.

Table 1.7: Summary of Characteristics of the Potentially Lethal Employee

Characteristic or Behavioral Warning Sign	Probability or Frequency
Male	80% - 95%
White	70%
Age range of 30 to 60 years.	75%
Exhibits significant social isolation.	50%
Experiences one or more triggering events within one year preceding the commission of the crime.	75% - 90%
Will vocalize or act out intentions before committing to violence.	frequency = common
Exhibits strange, threatening, or uncomfortable behavior that is observed by coworkers or supervisors over a period of time.	frequency = common
Will exhibit one behavioral warning sign.	90%
Will exhibit two or more behavioral warning signs.	50%
• history of violent behavior	frequency = common
• evidence of psychosis or severe psychological disorder	frequency = unknown
• obsession with another individual, evidence of romance obsession, or evidence of a severe delusional disorder that results in obsession with another individual	frequency = neutral in cases of multiple homicide, common in cases of individual homicide
• alcohol or chemical dependence	frequency = unknown but presumed to be common
• severe or chronic depression	frequency = common
• pathological blaming of others	frequency = common
• impaired neurological functioning	frequency = uncommon
• chronic or severely elevated frustration levels	frequency = common
• preoccupation with weapons, paramilitary or publicized incidents of violence in the workplace	frequency = common
• evidence of severe personality disorder	frequency = unknown

When the behavior of a known coworker changes significantly and the change is clearly not transitory, this is evidence that the individual is in need of assistance. The recognition of changing behavior that indicates the need for employee support must occur early in the behavioral escalation process and be followed quickly with intervention services such as counseling, medical assistance, or participation in an employee assistance program. Although few workers become lethal, many become violent. If coworkers and supervisors are able to recognize the early warning signs of violence and arrange for prompt intervention, it should be possible to eliminate much of the violence that now permeates many American work environments.

Here are some key indicators that may be exhibited by an employee whose behavior has begun to escalate toward aggression or violence. These can be considered as evidence of the need for intervention by a counselor, medical professional, or employee assistance program:

1. A pattern of obvious frustration accompanied by persistent blaming or unwarranted criticism of the organization, supervisors, or coworkers. This behavior may begin in a subtle, nonthreatening way and escalate in tone and vehemence. Should this behavior become evident in a worker who has no unusual history of frustrations, blaming, or criticism, it is of particular importance to provide positive intervention as quickly as possible. The potential for a violent reaction increases with the duration of the frustrations in evidence.
2. Unexplained, persistent, and abrupt changes in mood that persist over time.
3. Evidence of depression, increased social withdrawal, or avoidance of the usual workplace socialization in an employee who has not demonstrated this behavior previously.
4. Unprovoked outbursts of anger or aggression that are clearly inappropriate to the circumstances.
5. A significant and persistent change in work habits such as (a) a pattern of arriving late or being absent from work by an employee who has previously not demonstrated this behavior, (b) significant and prolonged deterioration in work performance by a reliable performer, (c) unexplained or vague illnesses or other physical deterioration in a previously healthy worker, or (d) avoidance of job responsibilities or disinterest in work exhibited by an employee who has been traditionally responsible and involved in workplace routines.
6. Evidence of substance or alcohol abuse.
7. A refusal to follow reasonable work directives, a significant increase in work errors, disregard of safety and security policies, or any similar behavior that may indicate that the worker is subject to undue stress. This is particularly significant if exhibited by an employee who has historically not exhibited signs of stress.
8. Bizarre or outlandish behavior that has the effect of inducing discomfort or fear in coworkers.
9. Argumentative or combative behavior, particularly if exhibited by an employee who has no previous history of this kind of act.
10. Any act of physical aggression, workplace disruption or sexual harassment that threatens the safety or wellness of a coworker.
11. Persistent discussions that revolve around the subjects of weaponry, paramilitary themes, and, of most importance, publicized incidents of workplace violence or homicide.
12. Threatening or intimidating behavior directed at coworkers, supervisors or the organization.

It is important to keep in mind that these indicators are general and cannot, in and of themselves, be considered to predict violent behavior. They are, however, reliable symptoms of an employee who needs assistance and whose behavior, if not corrected, may eventually lead to violence.

NOTES

1. U. S. Department of Health and Human Services (USHHS), *Fatal Injuries to Workers in the United States, 1980-1989: A Decade of Surveillance*, USHHS/National Institute of Occupational Health and Safety, August 1993, xii.

2. Ibid., 29-337.

3. J. Windau and G. Toscano, "Murder Inc.—Homicide in the American Workplace," *Business and Society Review*, no. 89 (1994): 58.

4. R. Backman, *Violence and Theft in the Workplace*, U.S. Department of Justice, Bureau of Justice Statistics, 15 July 1994.

5. T. Stanley Duncan, "Death in the Office—Workplace Homicides," *Law Enforcement Bulletin*, 64, no. 4 (April 1995): 20-25.

6. J. A. Fox and J. Levin, *Overkill: Mass Murder and Serial Killing Exposed* (New York: Plenum Press, 1994), 166.

7. S. A. Baron and E. D. Wheeler, *Violence in Our Schools, Hospitals and Public Places* (Ventura, Calif.: Pathfinder, 1994).

8. H. H. Goldman, ed., *Review of General Psychiatry*. (Norwalk, Conn.: Appleton and Lange/Prentice Hall, 1988), 671.

9. American Psychiatric Association, *Diagnostic and Statistical Manual of Mental Disorders*, 4th ed. (1994), 273-274.

10. Ibid., 296-297.

11. Tim Trebilcock, "I Love You to Death," *Redbook*, 178, March 1992: 100.

12. *DSM IV*, 320-327.

13. *DSM IV*, 339-344

14. Fox and Levin, *Overkill*, 155.

15. *DSM IV*, 645-649.

16. Ibid., 650-654.

17. Fox and Levin, *Overkill*, 181.

2

Case Studies—A Decade of the Lethal Employee

The disadvantage of men not knowing the past is that they do not know the present. History is a hill or high point of vantage, from which alone men see the town in which they live or the age in which they are living.

—G. K. Chesterton
All I Survey

The legacy of workplace homicide committed by the lethal employee is characterized most profoundly by reference to its burgeoning history as reported in the press, television, and sporadic official or academic reports. It is a troublesome history, typically leaving the observer with persistent questions of why such incidents should occur with increasing frequency across this nation. Although it cannot be quantifiably categorized with such common violence as robbery or extortion, the fact that this crime accounts for nearly one-fifth of all deaths in the workplace each year raises grave concerns about the safety of the work environment as well as what this trend means for all employees in the future. Supervisors are slain for actions consistent with their job responsibilities, and employees are murdered for reasons that are completely unclear or simply because they were in the wrong place at the wrong time. Victims are sometimes randomly targeted for what seems to be a symbolic and senseless motive in complete disregard of their humanity. Occupational homicide in any circumstance is heinous, but when the perpetrator is an employee, it is even more horrendous and inexcusable. It is the betrayal of a workplace trust that, until the past decade, had been a proud national tradition.

While major crime has decreased in many geographical areas of this nation during the past two years, this category of crime continues to defy an otherwise positive trend. The workplace murderer has become an established threat to all employees, supervisors, and clients. Even a cursory review of a decade of this crime supports the argument that workplace homicide stands alone as a unique and horrifying form of violence that is difficult to predict and often thwarts even sophisticated methods of prevention or intervention. In many ways, this crime defies understanding because it is so difficult to accept. Indeed, it is, overwhelmingly, an unacceptable betrayal of trust.

Excluding acts of terrorism and focusing on the traditional definition of occupational homicide, it is likely that well over 1,000 American workers will be slain this year—and that estimate may be conservative. Most of these workers will be slain in the course of another crime; yet, many will die at the hands of coworkers or former coworkers. The wave of workplace homicides, which first came to the public attention in 1986, continues unabated ten years later. The American worker and supervisor remain generally unprepared; they are hindered by a lack of understanding of the crime and its perpetrator and made vulnerable by the absence of prevention and intervention programs in most organizations. Compounding the issue is the common misperception that the devastating impact of a workplace murder is a distant and improbable threat, a freak occurrence unlikely to strike close to home. Clearly, with the victim count increasing every year, this is not only a false concept of security but a rapidly diminishing argument for the safety of the workplace.

It is difficult to both quantify a decade of workplace homicides and address the need for understanding of the crime and its perpetrator without sacrificing content for sensationalism. It is crucial that the motives and behavior of the potentially lethal employee be understood with sufficient detail that prevention becomes a real possibility in the workplace of the future. This is best accomplished by a detailed analysis of the crime and a comprehensive understanding of the perpetrator who commits it. The lethal employee has been holding the American workplace hostage for a decade, and it is unlikely he will fade away without strenuous efforts to understand why he acts out his aggressions with such vehemence and devastation.

One way of approaching a possible avenue of prevention is to review, and understand, key incidents of workplace murder committed by lethal employees. It is only possible to select a small number of the many incidents of workplace homicide that have occurred; each should stand the test of objectivity and be of sufficient detail to provide a practical level of understanding of the crime and its perpetrator. The compilation of incidents that follows is intended to do just that: to present a cross-section of the realities of workplace homicide committed by the lethal employee while lending some insight into the behavioral patterns that may have been critical to his eventual decision to kill. However, such a brief examination cannot possibly exhaust the issue or provide more than a preliminary basis for understanding and education—the crime is too complex for such a simple tactic. Like the exercise of profiling a potentially lethal employee, an understanding of the crime and its perpetrator cannot be completed with an incomplete history. One of the most troubling aspects of the crime, and one that compounds its incomplete history, is that it is rarely a predictable event, subject to cool analysis and scientific precision. Rather, it is, by definition, an event of chaotic and often indescribable consequences.

Finally, it must be strongly emphasized that there is no certain way of knowing when, or if, an employee will become lethal. There is only the possibility of refining future prevention methodologies by understanding historical incidents. Hopefully, as more is learned about the motives and behavior of the potentially lethal employee, the history of the crime itself will, someday, become an important component of effective prevention through understanding.

THE AWAKENING

Prior to 1986, Americans were largely unaware of the potential impact of workplace violence. That is not to say that the American workplace was free from crime or violence—it was not. However, violence in the workplace was generally handled within the structure of the organization itself, as a personnel issue, or as a matter for law enforcement. The increased rate and impact of crimes related to violence in the workplace was not viewed as categorical but rather as an extension of the overall increase of crime in society which was evident in the mid-1980s throughout America.

The phenomenon of occupational homicide was publicly unrecognized as a categorical criminal issue prior to the events in Edmond, Oklahoma, on August 20, 1986. Certainly, there had been many cases of occupational homicide prior to this, but they were not generally publicized in the national media, although a few of these incidents occurred in metropolitan courthouses and did draw significant media attention. However, at the time of the Edmond tragedy, these incidents were typically viewed as isolated acts of terrorism or retribution, and not as the emergence of a new category of major crime.

The actions of Patrick Sherrill at the Edmond Post Office forever altered the traditional view of a safe workplace in America. His crime was so unexpected, and so heinous, that it changed the long-standing definition of the American workplace and how it was viewed by employees in both the public and private sectors. In great measure, the actions of Patrick Sherrill introduced the unsettling concepts of workplace violence and the workplace murderer into the vocabulary of millions of Americans.

The Crime

The town of Edmond lies just north of Oklahoma City in the central part of the state. A suburb to its southerly neighbor, Edmond is a peaceful place with comfortable side streets and a relaxed, friendly pace of life. The town is obvious in its family orientation, offering pleasant, affordable housing and a variety of jobs for its residents. The Edmond Post Office is a sprawling and busy facility that serves thousands of the residents and businesses in, and around, Oklahoma City; it is an easily recognized landmark in town and major employer in Edmond. In every way, this suburban town represents the prototypical mid-American community, offering an excellent lifestyle, safety for its citizens, and job opportunities with established employers such as the Edmond post office. Unfortunately, in 1986 this peaceful venue became the site of one of the most horrendous incidents of workplace homicide in American history (see Table 2.1).

Table 2.1: Synopsis of Case Study No. 1

Perpetrator:	Patrick Henry Sherrill
Age:	44
Family:	Single
Date of Incident:	August 20, 1986
Location of Incident:	Edmond Post Office (Edmond, OK)
Employment Status:	Employed at the Edmond Post Office for less than 2 years.
Work History:	Held several previous jobs, possibly with questionable work performance.
Criminal History:	None
Fatalities and Injuries:	15 killed, 6 injured
	Perpetrator committed suicide at the scene.

Early on the morning of August 20, 1986, Patrick Sherrill, a full-time substitute letter carrier assigned to the Edmond Post Office, prepared a quick breakfast of scrambled eggs and set off for work, reporting in before 7:00 a.m. He was wearing the traditional uniform of a blue shirt and shorts and carrying a mailbag over his shoulder. However, on this morning his mailbag concealed two .45-caliber pistols, a .22-caliber handgun, and in excess of 300 rounds of ammunition. Sherrill, a member of the Oklahoma National Guard marksmanship team, had borrowed the two larger handguns and much of the ammunition from the guard armory. It was one of the benefits of having a proven skill with weapons which was granted to members of the guard marksmanship team. The .22-caliber handgun was his own property.

Sherrill entered the post office work area and strode quickly up to the shift supervisor, Richard Esser, Jr. Without speaking a word, he removed one of the powerful, .45-caliber weapons from his mailbag and pulled the trigger, shooting Esser point-blank in the chest and killing him instantly. Without pausing for a moment, Sherrill began wandering the hallways of the post office firing randomly at other employees. Any coworker unfortunate enough to be in Sherrill's proximity became a potential victim. In under ten minutes he managed to fire off more than fifty rounds of ammunition, killing fourteen of his coworkers at the scene, and injuring another six. Many of the fourteen people who were slain, like Richard Esser, were shot at point-blank range in the chest and quickly died at the scene from their massive wounds. Others, reacting to the surrounding mayhem, were shot trying to escape from their work areas. At the end of his rampage, Sherrill turned one of the handguns on himself and committed suicide. He died less than two feet from his first victim, and his primary target, Richard Esser, Jr. Sherrill had been working for the post office about sixteen months on the day he died.

Patrick Sherrill already lay dead on the floor of the post office when the Edmond Special Weapons and Tactics (SWAT) team arrived on the scene. For some forty-five minutes law enforcement officials tried to communicate with those inside the post office, both by bullhorn and by telephone. However, they received no response. Finally, at about 8:30 a.m., members of the SWAT team rushed the post office, where they found the bodies of Patrick Sherrill's fourteen victims, his own, and several seriously wounded employees.[1] The crime scene was horrendous and completely unexpected by even the seasoned law enforcement officers and emergency aid personnel.

When witnesses were interviewed after the murders, accusations and blame were rampant; everyone interviewed by the press had a notion of what went wrong, but very few of those who actually knew Sherrill agreed upon his motives. Some union officials blamed the killings on a tyrannical management style which, they claimed, was pervasive at the U.S. Postal Service. Managers on the scene said this simply was not true: the working environment was on a par with any other. Several officials claimed that Sherrill exhibited no warning signs of what was to come and said they were completely shocked by the events of that day. A few coworkers claimed Sherrill's actions were motivated by desires for revenge and a deep resentment against his shift supervisor, Richard Esser, Jr.; many others, profoundly distraught at what they had witnessed, simply refused to believe a person like Patrick Sherrill could have become a mass murderer at *their* workplace. Other individuals who knew Sherrill from his neighborhood claimed he was a polite man but a loner with some strange habits; several coworkers believed he was a troubled employee from the day he first started working at the Edmond Post Office.

Investigators combed through Patrick Sherrill's home in an effort to learn something of his motives. According to what they discovered, he had an obvious and strong interest in weapons and paramilitary themes. Sherrill's house was filled with copies of Soldier of Fortune magazine, many sets of camouflage outfits, and dozens of targets (some of human silhouettes) attached to walls or pasted to boxes. Other paramilitary paraphernalia was strewn about the house. It soon became clear that Sherrill had been preoccupied with themes of weaponry and the paramilitary for some time before his August rampage. However, none of his coworkers or neighbors had reported that Sherrill threatened others with his weapons or even discussed these ominous subjects in an unusual way. In fact, his coworkers and neighbors frequently recounted that he rarely socialized with anyone in the workplace or the neighborhood, at all.[2]

It would take many months before enough was learned about the incident at the Edmond Post Office to put the matter into some perspective. The crime was too unexpected and horrible to be easily accepted or coldly analyzed for some time. Sadly, for over two dozen of Patrick Sherrill's victims, there could never again be an opportunity for understanding. For many, and perhaps most, individuals in the American workforce, the ideal of a safe workplace was shattered as sensational reports of the murders spread throughout the nation. In less than ten minutes, Patrick Sherrill became one of the most prolific mass murderers in American history and the prototype of the lethal employee, changing forever the meaning of a safe workplace.[i]

The Perpetrator

At the time of the murders Patrick Sherrill was forty-four years old. He had lived with his mother most of his life, until she died in 1974. For twenty years prior to the shootings, Sherrill lived in the same house in Oklahoma City, keeping mostly to himself and socializing only with his mother while she was alive. Thereafter, he was completely alone. By all accounts he was socially isolated and withdrawn.

Patrick Sherrill's neighbors held several different views of him. Some of them called him "Crazy Pat" behind his back and accused him of peering into their windows at all hours of the night, dressed in combat fatigues. It was rumored throughout the neighborhood that Sherrill had some peculiar habits, like mowing his lawn at midnight and occasionally tying up the stray neighborhood dogs with bailing wire. Some of Sherrill's neighbors said he was just a loner with a few strange ways about him and that the neighborhood was awash in gossip. He was, however, generally considered polite and courteous to those around him—even helpful to others when it was needed. Sherrill was, in fact, an enigma to those who lived nearby; he was not well known to anyone. That he was considered somewhat strange by his neighbors never resulted in any action against him, criminal or otherwise.

The opinions of Sherrill's coworkers was somewhat different and more consistent with his eventual crime. He was generally viewed as a man who was often depressed at work and, at times, angry. Some coworkers saw him as a problem employee who was prone to poor performance and habitual complaining. It was generally agreed that he had no close friends and rarely, if ever, partook in the usual workplace socialization. According to reports of employees after the murders, Patrick Sherrill made some of his coworkers nervous and uncomfortable; none, however, reported having been in fear for their life, harassed, or intimidated by him.

Prior to joining the Edmond Post Office, Sherrill had a spotty job history. He was a marine on active duty during the Vietnam War but never saw combat.

---

i. Patrick Sherrill's actions in 1986 made him, at the time, the third worst mass murderer in American history.

Stationed at Camp LeJeune, North Carolina, for most of his three-year tour of duty, Sherrill achieved special recognition as a sharpshooter before he left the marines in 1966. He was both comfortable and familiar with handguns, collecting them personally and continuing an avid interest in weaponry and paramilitary themes once he returned to civilian life. After his discharge, Sherrill held a number of short-term jobs as a file clerk, stockroom worker, and bicycle repairman. In 1984, he joined the Oklahoma National Guard and, because of his skill with weapons, was made an instructor in the use of handguns and a key member of the marksmanship team. This gave him the ability to check weapons and ammunition out of the guard armory whenever he wished to do so. There was nothing unusual about this practice; Sherrill was a trusted member of the guard with a good performance record.

Patrick Sherrill was never married and had no criminal history. The only relative with whom he had close contact was his mother, until her death a dozen years before the post office shootings. His military record indicated no behavioral problems and no arrests or demotions while with the marines. Sherrill's performance as a file clerk, stockroom worker, and bicycle repairman was unknown.

While at the Edmond Post Office, Sherrill experienced some work performance difficulties, which were the subject of conversations with his supervisors and union representatives. Apparently these work performance problems were not considered serious by his supervisors. Officials at the post office claimed there were no plans to terminate Sherrill, although there was evidence that he had exhibited a continuing series of minor performance problems such as difficulty sorting mail properly and arriving late for work. The night before Patrick Sherrill's murderous rampage he discussed the possibility of a transfer to another post office with a union representative. It was uncertain if Sherrill faced any formal disciplinary action at work, but there is no evidence to indicate this as a possible motive. In fact, if there was a specific motivating factor that triggered Patrick Sherrill's actions on August 20, 1986, it has never been brought to light or substantiated. One can only assume that at least one motivating factor was job performance-related because of Sherrill's obvious targeting of the shift supervisor. However, this alone cannot explain his random execution of so many coworkers.

Analysis

Patrick Sherrill clearly exhibited several of the behavioral warning signs that are now associated with the potentially lethal employee (see Table 2.2). Unfortunately, in 1986, these behavioral characteristics were viewed quite differently than they are today. They may have been perceived as performance-related issues or distasteful personality characteristics; they were, most likely, not seen as indicators of potential violence. Perhaps they were not considered at all. There would have been little reason to be concerned with the possibility of mass murder in the workplace at that time and in that environment. However, as the history of occupational homicide has demonstrated, Sherrill's behavior, personal characteristics, and actions proved, in retrospect, to be prototypical for what is now recognized as a major threat to any American workplace.

Sherrill was a solitary, mid-forties male who collected weapons, exhibited an abiding interest in paramilitary subjects, was proficient in the use of firearms, and had easy access to them. He was apparently frustrated and angry at work, and he may have been suffering from depression. Sherrill had few if any friends and lived completely alone after the death of his mother. Reports of Sherrill's performance at work varied considerably, but they were generally somewhat negative. At the time of the murders, some press reports asserted that he was a perpetually troubled employee who was the target of disciplinary action by post office supervisors. Other reports described his workplace difficulties in milder terms. By any account, however, it is reasonable to assume that Patrick Sherrill had, at the least, a somewhat troubled pattern of work history and performance. He had held several low-paying jobs for relatively short periods of time and had been at the Edmond Post Office less than two years before the shootings. Despite his short tenure at the post office, there were concerns about his performance from several quarters. This, in combination with Sherrill's behavioral profile, would be considered a significant behavioral warning sign today.

Patrick Sherrill exhibited behavior indicative of a man prone to violence. Although there is no evidence of a history of violence, he was clearly equipped with lethal weapons and was an expert in their use. He was passionately interested in themes involving weapons and may have been obsessed with the subject. As a frustrated individual, suffering difficulties at work and with no significant individual to whom he could reach out when in need, Sherrill could be considered a potentially dangerous employee. Compounding these warning signs was the possibility of a depression disorder, potentially serious in nature, which would imply an increased level of danger to himself and others. Given the pattern of his life and, in particular, his behavior prior to the killings, Sherrill may have suffered from one or more major depressive episodes throughout his adulthood.

It can be reasonably assumed that Patrick Sherrill specifically targeted his shift supervisor, Richard Esser, Jr., as a primary victim in his murderous rampage. The fact that Sherrill attacked Esser first, at point-blank range, is an indication that his first victim may not have been selected at random. His actions after that, however, were clearly indiscriminate and probably symbolic. Patrick Sherrill killed randomly in an apparent (symbolic) attempt to destroy the real target of his revenge—his employer. He probably gave little thought to the individuals he killed and may have been nearly, or completely, dissociated from his actions and their impact. Having completed his mission or, perhaps, realizing the horrifying result of his actions, Sherrill ended his rampage in a final—perhaps also symbolic—act of suicide.

When evaluating Patrick Sherrill in terms of the working profile of a potentially lethal employee, it can be seen why he is considered prototypical:

1. Sherrill exhibited several of the personal characteristics of the potentially lethal employee, including sex, age grouping, ethnicity, and social isolation.
2. He exhibited several key behavioral warning signs indicative of potential violence: a preoccupation with weapons and paramilitary themes (evident from the post-incident investigation), severe or chronic depression (probable, based on his lifestyle and the reports of coworkers and neighbors), and severe or chronic frustration (possible, indicated by job history and the reports of coworkers and supervisors).

Finally, Patrick Sherrill had ready access to weapons and expert knowledge in their use. This combination of factors constitutes, in retrospect, a high probability of violence—an eventuality that no one at the Edmond Post Office had reason to suspect at that time.

Table 2.2: Summary of Characteristics: Patrick Sherrill

Male:	yes
Age range of 30-60 years:	yes
Evidence of social isolation:	yes
Evidence of triggering events:	uncertain
Vocalized violent intentions:	no
Exhibited behavior uncomfortable to coworkers:	yes
History of violent behavior:	no
Evidence of psychosis or psychological disorder:	no
Evidence of obsession or delusional disorder:	no
Alcohol or chemical dependence:	no
Severe or chronic depression:	possible
Pathological blaming:	possible
Impaired neurological functioning:	no
Chronic or severe frustration:	possible
Preoccupation with weapons or paramilitary themes:	yes
Evidence of severe personality disorder:	no

DEATH IN THE SKIES

There are few acts of workplace murder more horrible than those committed by David Burke (see Table 2.3). Nearly all the individuals killed in this incident had absolutely no connection with Burke and, in fact, did not even know his name. Burke sought revenge against a former supervisor who had played a key role in the termination from a job he held for thirteen years. However, his anger was uncontrolled and his vehemence unchecked, resulting in the deaths of over forty innocent individuals. Although indiscriminate killing is not uncommon for the lethal employee, the extent and methodology of David Burke's revenge remains unparalleled.

Table 2.3: Synopsis of Case Study No. 2

Perpetrator:	David Burke
Age:	35
Family:	Unmarried (father of seven children)
Date of Incident:	December 9, 1987
Location of Incident:	Airborne near San Luis Obispo, CA.
Employment Status:	Terminated after 13 years of service with USAir and PSA.
Work History:	Stable with apparently satisfactory performance.
Criminal History:	Investigated while working in New York but no charges were ever filed.
Fatalities and Injuries:	43 killed, no survivors
	Perpetrator was killed with his victims in airplane crash.

The Crime

David Burke worked for USAir, the parent company of Pacific Southwest Airlines (PSA), in the Rochester, New York, office for thirteen years before moving to California to join PSA as a ticket agent in Los Angeles. In November 1987, Burke was accused of stealing $69 from in-flight cocktail receipts after security personnel reviewed a routine videotape of employee activities. The tape clearly showed Burke stealing the cash, and he never disputed the charges when confronted with them. He did, however, ask for leniency for his children in an effort to keep his position, but to no avail. On November 19, 1987, David Burke was fired from his job by Raymond Thompson, the USAir customer-service manager in Los Angeles.[3]

On learning of his termination, Burke became angry and violent, threatening Thompson and others. A few days after being fired, he held a female companion and her six-year-old daughter hostage at gunpoint for over six hours, forcing them to drive aimlessly around the Los Angeles basin. At home and to his few friends, Burke persistently vocalized threats against USAir, PSA, and his former supervisor, Raymond Thompson. Those close to him described Burke in the weeks following the loss of his job as furious and out of control.

On December 9, 1987, David Burke boarded PSA flight 1771, which originated in San Diego with a stopover in Los Angeles and a final destination of San Francisco. Despite the fact Burke was no longer an airline employee, he still had possession of his PSA identification card and was able to board the flight without passing through the usual airport security checkpoints. Burke knew that Raymond Thompson would also be onboard this flight, as it was a regular commute schedule that the PSA supervisor had used for years. Burke was well prepared for a final act of revenge. Two weeks previously, he had borrowed a .44-magnum revolver from another USAir employee, and now he had no difficulty smuggling the handgun aboard the flight as he bypassed airport metal detectors using his employee identification.

Once airborne, Burke removed an air sickness bag from the pocket of the seat in front of him and wrote a final message to Raymond Thompson: "Hi, Ray. I think it's sort of ironical that we end up like this. I asked for some leniency for my family, remember. Well I got none and you'll get none."[4] Flight 1771 was, by this time, at 22,000 feet, nearing San Luis Obispo. What then transpired was later re-created from radio conversations and the Federal Aviation Administration (FAA)-required cockpit-recording device carried by all commercial airlines.

Burke moved forward in the cabin of the airliner to where Thompson was sitting. He fired two shots at his former supervisor, probably killing him where he sat. An airline attendant was heard saying, "We've got a problem here," immediately followed by a male voice (that of David Burke) responding, "I'm the problem!"[5] The pilot, hearing the commotion in the cabin and the flight attendant's warning, started an emergency transmission to air-traffic controllers with the message, "Seven-seven-zero-zero"—the code for an emergency on board. A few seconds later he radioed, "I have an emergency . . . gunfire!"[6] The cockpit recorder then picked up the sounds of a struggle on the flight deck followed by a series of gunshots. David Burke had shot the entire flight crew, causing the airliner to pitch into a steep dive, out of control. Within two minutes of the first warning, Flight 1771 plummeted in a near-vertical trajectory, from an altitude of four miles, into a muddy pasture near San Luis Obispo. All forty-three individuals onboard perished.

Combing the wreckage, FBI and local law enforcement officials were able to recover the handgun used by David Burke. It contained six spent cartridges. They also discovered the note written to Raymond Thompson, the intact flight recorder, the bodies of both men, and the remains of more than forty innocent individuals. The following day, volunteer workers, still combing the scene, located the identification badge David Burke had used to board the PSA flight. Given the evidence at the crash site, the radio transmissions in the last few moments of flight, and the information on the cockpit recorder, the FBI was able to re-create the final, horrible moments of Flight 1771. It was clear that David Burke had planned the execution of Raymond Thompson, himself, and whoever else might stand between them, regardless of the consequences. With this unspeakable crime of mass murder David Burke became the most lethal employee in American history at that time.

The Perpetrator

David Burke was born to Jamaican parents in Britain, emigrating to the United States as a young adult. Although he never married, by the time Burke was in his thirties he had fathered seven children by four different women. Despite the fact Burke was considered a genial, hard-working individual by most of his coworkers, to his friends he was known as a man with a hair-trigger temper (see Table 2.4). When Burke lived and worked in New York, he had been investigated for selling drugs, automobile theft, and insurance fraud; however, no charges were ever filed against him. Burke's work history was stable, with no apparent performance difficulties. Some of David Burke's friends described him as aggressive and unpredictably violent yet obviously concerned about his children. His activities indicate that he may have been habitually abusive to the women in his life and disdainful of others.

Table 2.4: Summary of Characteristics: David Burke

Male:	yes
Age range of 30-60 years:	yes
Evidence of social isolation:	somewhat
Evidence of triggering events:	yes
Vocalized violent intentions:	yes
Exhibited behavior uncomfortable to coworkers:	somewhat
History of violent behavior:	possible
Evidence of psychosis or psychological disorder:	possible
Evidence of obsession or delusional disorder:	no
Alcohol or chemical dependence:	no
Severe or chronic depression:	no
Pathological blaming:	possible
Impaired neurological functioning:	no
Chronic or severe frustration:	no
Preoccupation with weapons or paramilitary themes:	no
Evidence of severe personality disorder:	no

Burke seemed to move from relationship to relationship with little effort. Transferring from his home of over a decade in New York to Los Angeles left him more socially isolated than he had been before. This did not, however, prevent him from establishing new domestic arrangements. Shortly after arriving in California he entered into a relationship with another ticket agent who also worked for USAir. Just before boarding Flight 1771 he left this ominous message on her answering machine: "Jackie, this is David. I'm on my way to San Francisco, Flight 1771. I love you. I really wish I could say more, but I *do* love you." This is the same woman he had held hostage at gunpoint for over six hours just weeks previously. It was David Burke's final message to his family.

Although Burke had no criminal record, it is possible that he pushed the limits of legal behavior on a number of fronts. His domestic relationships were not stable, and law enforcement officials considered him to be involved in a variety of illegal activities. It is unclear why he left New York, but it is possible that he needed a change in venue for domestic or, possibly, legal reasons. Despite his generally mild reputation at work, Burke seemed to be a man whose life was characterized by unstable domestic relationships and questionable activities outside the work environment. That he had an unpredictable temper was obvious.

Analysis

David Burke's reaction to the triggering event of his termination was unbelievably extreme. His obvious intention was to exact the maximum possible revenge against his former employer as well as his supervisor. That he was willing to slaughter so many uninvolved, innocent individuals seems incomprehensible and speaks volumes about his disdain for others. It is clear that Burke considered the loss of his job as tantamount to the end of his life. His immediate reaction, to take the mother of one of his children hostage at gunpoint, seems not only inappropriate but also desperate and pathological. His notorious temper also indicates possible mental instability, while his brushes with the law indicate, at minimum, a disregard for the rights of others.

Although David Burke had no history of a mental disorder, this cannot be ruled out as a possible factor in his crime. His general behavior away from work was mildly antisocial, and his reactions to stressful events were clearly extreme and unpredictable. A question that can never be answered was whether or not Burke suffered from some psychological disorder that enabled his incredible act of violence. This seems a possibility.

The actions of the airline's management clearly facilitated David Burke's murderous reaction to his dismissal. It appears that the organization elected to immediately terminate Burke for petty theft without regard to his potentially violent reaction. Worse, airline management made no obvious effort to protect the workplace after Burke's termination. The fact that he was easily able to board an airliner using an invalid identification card and to avoid detection of a large handgun is painful testimony to the lack of security prevalent at that time. Regardless of whether or not one shares the view that the punishment for Burke's petty theft was extreme, the absence of reasonable efforts to secure the work environment from a potentially violent employee seems unforgivable and clearly negligent.

The heinous crime of David Burke remains unique in the history of occupational homicide; it was an incident that will hopefully never be repeated. The unspeakable horror that must have been experienced by the passengers and crew of Flight 1771 during the last few moments of life will forever remain an unforgettable testimony to the potential of the lethal employee and the need for employers to work diligently to prevent any possibility of similar incidents in the future.

AN OBSESSION WITH LAURA

Romance obsession, a type of delusional disorder sometimes referred to as *erotomania*, has received a good deal of attention in the media because of the stalking activities and violence committed against well-known public personalities. Cases like that of John Hinkley, who stalked and shot President Reagan in an effort to impress actress Jodi Foster, or Robert Bardo, who stalked and murdered actress Rebecca Schaeffer, tend to attract enduring attention in the press and on television. However, this form of aberrant behavior also occurs with surprising frequency in the workplace and, in some situations, can be the precursor to extreme violence. The case of Richard Farley's complete obsession with a coworker, Laura Black, vividly exemplifies the kind of ultimate violence that can result from such a particularly virulent delusional disorder (see Table 2.5).

Table 2.5: Synopsis of Case Study No. 3

Perpetrator:	Richard Wade Farley
Age:	39
Family:	Single (lived with a girlfriend for a short period).
Date of Incident:	February 16, 1988
Location of Incident:	ESL Incorporated (Sunnyvale, CA)
Employment Status:	Terminated in 1986 after 4 years of service.
Work History:	Questionable work history. Terminated for threatening a coworker.
Criminal History:	None
Fatalities and Injuries:	7 killed, 4 injured
	Perpetrator survived his crime. Sentenced to death on January 17, 1992.

The Crime

By the 1980s, Electromagnetic Systems Labs (ESL) Incorporated could be justifiably proud of its reputation as a premier defense contractor and a respected landmark in the burgeoning electronics industry. Located in the heart of Silicon Valley, with a modern office complex in the flourishing city of Sunnyvale, ESL provided its employees with a comfortable working environment and a camaraderie unique to the high-tech firms that populated the area south of San Francisco known as the Peninsula. It was, by any standard, an exciting place to work, located in an area of California known for its singular blend of relaxed living, unparalleled business innovations, and modern management styles. It was into this environment that Richard Wade

Farley would arrive as a software technician in search of the consummate career.

There would have been every reason for Farley to look forward to the future with unrestrained optimism when he joined the company after leaving the military. This was, after all, a nearly ideal turn of circumstances for a man with a much-demanded skill and a high security clearance gained from a ten-year stint with the navy. Still, Richard Farley reported to work that first day with something dark and unseen secreted within his psyche. Perhaps he sensed his own uneasiness; or maybe he dismissed it as the expected initial jitters of beginning a new and challenging career. Perhaps he never felt anything at all. Whatever he may have known or expected, in less than four years, Farley would leave this company and its employees forever changed; they would be permanently scarred by the unrecognized, but developing, psychosis that he brought to ESL that day. His legacy would be one of unforgettable mayhem— that of one of California's most vicious workplace murderers.

From the moment Farley was introduced to Laura Black, an electrical engineer who had worked at the company for less than a year, he was obsessed with her. The dark-haired and athletic twenty-two year-old spoke easily to him during that first meeting, unaware that Richard Farley had already decided he would have her, one way or the other. Later, when recalling their first meeting during court testimony, Farley said: "I think I fell instantly in love with her. It was just one of those things, I guess." Laura Black, at first, had no inkling of Richard Farley's obsession with her.

During the three and a half years following that meeting, Farley would write some 200 letters to Black, constantly follow her to and from work, leave gifts on her desk, and rifle through confidential personnel files to learn more about her personal life. At one point, learning that Black was to visit her parents in Virginia in December 1984, Farley broke into her desk at the office, obtained the address of her parents, and then wrote letters to her in Virginia.[7] Throughout 1984 and 1985, his letters were not overtly threatening, but that was to change as Laura continued to thwart his advances.

Farley would frequently drive past Black's home at night, telephone her at any hour, and, at one point, even joined her aerobics class to remain as close as possible to her, day and night. Although Richard Farley dated another woman, with whom he eventually lived in his San Jose bungalow, he twice attempted to move into the apartment building where Black lived. When at work or approaching her on the street, Farley would often ask for a date but would inevitably be turned aside by the polite and naturally gentle woman. These rejections would inevitably bring on recurring protestations and endless restatements of his limitless love for her. She did what she could to avoid him and deter his advances; he responded by redoubling his efforts with more telephone calls, more harassment, more gifts, and incessant car trips past her home. Laura Black was forced to move twice during these years as Farley's harassment continued unabated at work, at her apartment complex, and even on shopping trips.

Eventually, Richard Farley could no longer take "no" for an answer, and his tactics became aggressive and cruel. He would make derogatory statements about Laura and rifle through her locked desk in search of even more information about her personal life and activities away from work. It seemed that every effort Laura Black made to avoid Farley was answered with further encounters with him, each contact becoming more offensive than the previous. Richard Farley was a man who had obviously succumbed to an obsession, which was quickly approaching a violent finale. Laura Black was running out of options; her life had become hell thanks to Richard Farley.

By the fall of 1985, Richard Farley had pursued Laura Black so vehemently that she turned to the human resources department at ESL for help. Farley was told he must attend psychological counseling sessions and stop harassing Black if he wanted to keep his job.[8] Although Farley attended the required counseling sessions on a regular schedule, the harassment did not diminish—rather, it escalated. During the period he was attending counseling, Farley made a duplicate copy of Laura Black's house key, which she had inadvertently left on her desk. Rather than using the key to gain entry to her apartment, Farley displayed the key and a handwritten note on the dashboard of his car so that Black, and others, would know he could get to her at any time. His driving excursions past her home and his late-night telephone calls to her increased. The letters he wrote to Black became more threatening, sometimes referring to his large gun collection.

Finally, in 1986, Farley could no longer control his growing anger at Black's continuing rejections. He publicly and vehemently threatened her life if she would not submit to his desire to have her for himself. Farley also began threatening other employees at the company, including a manager, whom he warned about his gun collection, his expertise with guns, and the fact that he "could take people with [him]" if provoked.[9] ESL management, which was by now very concerned about Richard Farley's bizarre behavioral patterns, terminated him in May 1986. They were clearly concerned about Laura Black's safety as well as that of others in organization. Even as Farley was being fired from his job, an ESL manager warned Black once more about his uncontrollable obsession and the company's concern for her safety. Still, even termination from his $36,000-a-year position could not dissuade Farley. In fact, in a letter he penned to Black just before he was fired from his job, Farley wrote: "Once I'm fired, you won't be able to control me ever again. Pretty soon, I'll crack under the pressure and run amok and destroy everything in my path."[10] His words proved prophetic in the extreme.

For the next year and a half Richard Farley continued to harass Laura Black. He was experiencing economic hardships, lost two houses, and found himself in trouble with the Internal Revenue Service (IRS) for back taxes. However, none of this seemed to matter to Farley. He thought constantly about Laura Black and increased his efforts to gain her affection. The fact that he could no longer see her at work did nothing to check his pursuit. The telephone calls continued, as did his habit of following her whenever he could. By

November 1987, his letters to Black were voluminous and overtly threatening. In that month he wrote: "You cost me a job, forty thousand dollars in equity taxes I can't pay, and a foreclosure. Yet I still like you. Why do you want to find out how far I'll go?"[11] Closing his letter, Farley threatened Black again: "I absolutely will not be pushed around, and I'm beginning to get tired of being nice."[12]

Laura Black, in fear for her life and completely victimized by the ever-present Farley, eventually sought, and was granted, a temporary restraining order (TRO) against him. The TRO forbade him from approaching within 300 yards of Black and ordered him not to contact her in any manner. The order was served against Richard Farley on February 8, 1988, with a hearing scheduled for the matter on February 17, 1988. For Farley, this temporary restraining order was an act of ultimate abandonment on Black's part. He now knew, without question, that she would never submit to his advances. All that was left for Richard Farley was revenge—and he already had much of what he needed to take that course. Still, on February 9, 1988, Richard Farley purchased a new, 12-gauge semiautomatic shotgun and ammunition for his arsenal of personal weapons. He spent $2,000 that day, despite his financial problems, just to be sure he had everything he needed.

When Farley returned to the offices of his former employer on Tuesday, February 16, 1988, he was clearly prepared for maximum violence. It was just after 3:00 p.m. as he drove his motor home into the ESL parking lot, armed with his new shotgun, a rifle, two handguns, bandoleers of ammunition strapped across his chest, and a container of gasoline.[13] In all, Richard Farley carried nearly one hundred pounds of firearms and ammunition, which he transferred from the motor home to his body in preparation for his planned assault on ESL.

Walking across the parking lot to the office building, Farley shot and killed his first victim, a forty-six-year-old data processing specialist whom he knew. He then approached the building entrance and blasted his way through the locked glass doors, heading directly for Laura Black's office. Making his way to Black's location, Farley fired indiscriminately at anyone in his path. Before reaching Black, Farley shot six employees, killing four instantly with powerful blasts from his semiautomatic shotgun. Hearing the chaos outside of her office, Laura Black slammed and locked the door, hoping to find some refuge.

It was to no avail. Farley leveled his shotgun at the office door and blew it off the hinges. Jumping past the shattered door and moving swiftly towards Black's desk, he raised the shotgun again and fired twice. The first shot missed, but the second critically wounded Black, severing arteries, tearing muscles, and destroying the bone in her shoulder. Although losing a great deal of blood and in unimaginable pain, Black was able to avoid Farley by hiding in an adjoining office and then making a run for the parking lot where, by that time, waiting ambulances and a SWAT team had arrived.

During his rampage Farley killed seven employees and wounded another four, including Black. At the end of his murderous siege, which lasted for five hours, Farley surrendered to a police SWAT team. Throughout the standoff (as law enforcement personnel later recounted), Richard Farley expressed no remorse for what he had done and, in fact, appeared to delight in the mayhem and chaos surrounding his actions. The once pristine ESL offices had become a chaotic killing zone of the dead and wounded. Videos and photographs of the events that day clearly depict the heroic efforts of law enforcement officials helping those employees fortunate enough to escape Farley's revenge as they scurried for any cover they could find. The injured, including a critically wounded Laura Black, were rushed away for treatment as members of the SWAT team eventually ushered Richard Farley from ESL for the final time.

The day after Farley's rampage, Family Court Commissioner Lois Kittle declared the restraining order obtained by Laura Black a few weeks earlier as permanent. It was clearly a symbolic, but important, act. A tearful Commissioner Kittle, in making her pronouncement, said, "Pieces of paper do not stop bullets."[14] On that day it was uncertain whether Laura Black would survive to testify against Richard Wade Farley.

Farley went on trial in 1991, charged with seven counts of capital murder and four additional felonies. In his testimony Farley admitted that he knew he should not have harassed Laura Black but claimed he could not help himself. He argued that he had instantly fallen in love with his former coworker, saying, "The more she tries to push me away, the more I try to not have her push me away."[15] According to his testimony, Ms. Black's final response to his incessant attempts to date her was that she would not go out with him even if, "I was the last man on Earth."[16] During the course of the trial, Laura Black, still in obvious pain from her injuries, was able to testify that she had not encouraged Farley in any way and rather had, in fact, made extraordinary efforts to avoid him and deter his advances. Having been grievously wounded during the siege of February 16, 1988, Black made a compelling witness against the remorseless Farley. It was clear she had truly been persecuted by Richard Farley.

During closing arguments, Farley's defense attorney, Gregory Paraskou, pleaded passionately for the life of his client, pointing out to the jury that Farley was "one of God's children" and should be spared the ultimate penalty for his crimes.[17] Assistant District Attorney Charles Constantinides countered with the argument that Richard Farley had obviously targeted his victims without passion and in a manner that indicated no regard for human life. Constantinides reminded the jury that Farley had made sure several of his victims were dead by shooting them in the back at near point-blank range with his shotgun and also recalled Farley's statement after the murders that he would "smile for the cameras" if he should be sentenced to the gas chamber.[18]

On October 21, 1991, the jury found Richard Wade Farley guilty of seven counts of capital murder and four additional felonies. The following month, on November 1, 1991, the same jury, after only a single day of deliberation, recommended the death penalty.[19] On January 17, 1992, Superior Court Judge Joseph Biafore, Jr., sentenced Farley to death in the gas chamber. In passing the sentence, Judge Biafore described Farley as a vicious killer who demonstrated a "complete disregard for human life."[20] Richard Farley was remanded to San Quentin prison, north of San Francisco, to await his required appeals and eventual execution.

The incredible nightmare of Laura Black had finally reached a kind of conclusion, and in a legal sense, justice was served. However, for seven of Black's coworkers and friends, and for Laura Black herself, who was permanently disabled as a result of the vicious attack, there may never be a final and satisfactory resolution to the heinous crimes of Richard Wade Farley. His legacy remains vivid and horrific.

The Perpetrator

Richard Wade Farley was born in 1948, in Texas. He was the oldest of six children raised by an air force mechanic and his wife. During Farley's early years, the household moved frequently as the air force reassigned Richard's father. Later, the family settled in the small town of Petaluma, forty miles north of San Francisco.

Richard was an unremarkable and isolated child born to a family that was not close. When testifying in his defense, one of Richard's brothers stated that he had not talked to Richard in the ten years preceding the trial. In school, Richard was considered shy by his classmates and had no close friends. There were no known incidents of problems with the law or extreme behavior as the boy was growing. In fact, until the murders he committed in 1988, Richard had no criminal record whatsoever.

In 1966, Richard Farley attended community college but dropped out to join the navy the following year. While in the navy, Farley was trained in computer technology and earned awards for good conduct and marksmanship. Those who knew him, though, found him to be a loner, egotistical, and arrogant.

In 1977, Farley left the navy and purchased a small bungalow in San Jose, California—at the southern edge of the booming Silicon Valley. He later joined ESL to make use of the skills acquired in the navy and pursue a promising career within a reasonable commute from his home. By the early 1980s, Richard Farley was a pudgy, bespectacled man with a puffy face that was beginning to show an approach to middle age. He was also a collector of weapons and numerous books dealing with sex and violence.[21] All that was missing for Farley was an object for his latent, deadly obsession.

Analysis

Park E. Dietz, M.D., Ph.D., is an eminent forensic psychiatrist who is also a respected authority on mass murderers and stalkers. Dietz has defined three specific subtypes of the romantic stalker, which can be practically applied in an attempt to better understand the motivations of such a criminal:

1. The spurned ex-lover or spouse whose primary motivation is revenge against the person who has rejected or offended him or her.
2. The individual suffering from a delusional disorder who will engage in bizarre and clearly unrealistic fantasies, often believing he or she is involved in a love relationship with a prominent or symbolic individual.
3. The individual suffering from a pathological dependence on another who becomes obsessed with the target of his or her dependence and finds it difficult or impossible to function without the attention and companionship of that person.[22]

In Dietz's scenario, Richard Farley belongs to the last category.

Table 2.6: Summary of Characteristics: Richard Wade Farley

Male:	yes
Age range of 30-60 years:	yes
Evidence of social isolation:	some
Evidence of triggering events:	yes
Vocalized violent intentions:	yes
Exhibited behavior uncomfortable to coworkers:	yes
History of violent behavior:	no
Evidence of psychosis or psychological disorder:	no
Evidence of obsession or delusional disorder:	yes
Alcohol or chemical dependence:	no
Severe or chronic depression:	uncertain
Pathological blaming:	yes
Impaired neurological functioning:	no
Chronic or severe frustration:	yes
Preoccupation with weapons or paramilitary themes:	yes
Evidence of severe personality disorder:	possible

There are several variations of behavioral characteristics and criteria that can be broadly defined as *romance obsession* among the burgeoning incidents of workplace homicide available in the literature. From a formal, diagnostic point of view, romance obsession is considered to be a *delusional disorder* of the subtype *erotomanic*.[23] This disorder "often concerns idealized romantic love and spiritual union rather than sexual attraction"—a signification well suited to Richard Farley's obsession with Laura Black. On the other hand, the strict definition of this subtype, as offered by *DSM IV*, is that the disorder, "applies when the central theme of the delusion is that another person is in love with the individual"—a more specific interpretation, which cannot be attributed to Farley.[24] In the classical definition of delusional disorder, erotomanic type, the unwelcome behavior typically involves unsolicited and troublesome letters, telephone calls, gift giving, visits, and surveillance—all activities undertaken by Richard Farley. As to whether he was convinced that Laura Black was in love with him, there is much doubt. The evidence indicates that he was well aware Black had no romantic interest in him and, in fact, desired not to be approached by him in any manner. In the most strict interpretation provided by *DSM IV*, for lack of a more precise categorization, Richard Farley would be considered as suffering from a delusional disorder of the erotomanic type. From a less clinical viewpoint, Richard Farley was locked in a struggle for power with Laura Black. It was his clear and obvious intention to dominate Black, to have her for himself and himself alone. When he was unable to cajole, harass, or intimidate Black into submission, he made the conscious decision to murder her, along with whoever might stand between them. Such brutal actions, even though they may be predicated upon a well-defined delusional disorder, demonstrate obvious pathological behavior of the most extreme kind.

By Dietz's definitions, Richard Farley was an individual suffering from a pathological dependence on Laura Black—a diagnosis that is more appropriate to the facts of the case than the rather rigid *DSM IV* diagnosis of delusional disorder, erotomanic type.[25] Lending credence to the argument of pathological dependence is the account of Farley's behavior leading up to the murders. Much of this behavior is reminiscent of certain criteria of *dependent personality disorder* in relation to Laura Black.[26] Farley apparently had difficulty in managing his personal affairs because of his obsession, as evidenced by a significant deterioration in his financial condition; he was obviously in fear of driving Black away and consistently made great efforts to maintain some relationship with her, as evidenced by his actions; moreover, he went to excessive lengths to win her attention and felt helpless when he was unable to gain it, as evidenced by the content of many of the letters written to Laura Black. These behavioral characteristics are closely aligned with the classic criteria for dependent personality disorder. To complicate this pathologically dependent behavior, Farley demonstrated obvious traits of obsessive behavior which, in the end, deteriorated into threats and violence.

The categorizations used by Dietz fit well with many cases of occupational homicide where romance obsession is a clear theme. The application of Dietz's classifications to Richard Farley indicate that he suffered from a pathological dependence upon Laura Black combined with obsessive behavior. This diagnosis accounts well for his actions and provides a strong working analysis of this type of occupational homicide. When these behavioral characteristics were combined with Farley's fetish for weapons; his highly developed skill with a variety of firearms; additional personality traits, which included social avoidance and a strong sense of dissociation from others; it seems, in retrospect, all too obvious that he was a man quite capable of the extreme violence be wrought on Laura Black and her coworkers (see Table 2.6).

A MODEL EMPLOYEE

By all accounts, John Taylor was a model employee, who was popular with coworkers and neighbors. He had frequently won awards from his employer for outstanding performance and demonstrated a long and productive work history. Taylor was said to be deeply in love with his wife and well respected in the community. Nonetheless, John Taylor became both a domestic and workplace murderer, shocking and horrifying those who thought they knew him well (see Table 2.7).

Table 2.7: Synopsis of Case Study No. 4

Perpetrator:	John M. Taylor
Age:	51
Family:	Married. Murdered his wife on the date of the incident.
Date of Incident:	August 10, 1989
Location of Incident:	Orange Glen Post Office (CA)
Employment Status:	Employed at the Orange Glen Post Office for 27 years.
Work History:	Stable with good to excellent performance.
Criminal History:	None
Fatalities and Injuries:	3 killed (excluding Mrs. Taylor), 5 injured
	Perpetrator committed suicide at the scene.

The Crime

John Taylor worked for the U.S. Postal Service nearly all his adult life. He was considered an exemplary employee by his supervisors and coworkers, often receiving awards from management for superior performance and excellent customer service. By 1989, Taylor was celebrating his twenty-seventh year of service at the Orange Glen Post Office, located thirty-five miles north of San Diego.

Taylor was in the habit of reporting early to work so he could spend a few social moments with two coworkers he had known for many years. The three friends would gather each morning at a small table to have coffee and discuss the previous day's activities before setting off on their duties; it was a comfortable workplace ritual that had been carried on for years. On August 10, 1989, John Taylor arrived as usual to meet his coworkers. On this day, however, he carried a loaded .22-caliber, semiautomatic pistol and a box of one hundred rounds of ammunition with him. Taylor approached the table where his two friends were chatting and, without speaking a word, shot both of them to death. Entering through the side door of the station, Taylor then began roaming through the post office work area, firing his handgun at other employees.

During his short rampage, Taylor shot at some coworkers and bypassed others; it appeared he had no specific victims in mind, as he never singled out a supervisor or manager. Taylor did not utter a word throughout the shooting spree; witnesses among the horrified staff said his actions seemed to be completely indiscriminate. After firing off twenty rounds, John Taylor silently put the barrel of the gun to his own head and pulled the trigger, dying instantly at the scene.

When police investigated the incident at Orange Glen, they discovered that John Taylor had murdered his wife earlier that morning by shooting her twice in the head while she slept.

The Perpetrator

John Taylor was a most unlikely candidate as a lethal employee or even a violent individual. Married for over twenty years to the same woman, Taylor was considered to be a loving husband and excellent stepfather to his twenty-two-year-old stepson. Taylor's neighbors universally stated that he and Mrs. Taylor were constantly in each other's company and seemed to have an excellent relationship. To those who knew Taylor it seemed inconceivable that he could have harmed his wife or murdered anyone.

Taylor had no criminal record, no history of violence, and no obsession with weapons or paramilitary issues. He lived quietly with his wife and had a normal social life with friends in the neighborhood and at work. His reputation in the workplace and the neighborhood was generally impeccable. By all accounts, John Taylor was the least likely employee at the Orange Glen station to be a murderer. However, there *were* some questions—perhaps there were some indications that John Taylor was not the happy man he appeared to be.

For a few months preceding the murders, Taylor grumbled to others about his domestic situation. Coworkers recalled that this was unusual for Taylor, who had always expressed very positive sentiments about his marriage. Those who knew him agreed that it was odd for Taylor to complain about anything at all; they generally viewed his minor complaints about his marriage as not significant.

Then, there was the matter of workplace morale. John Taylor had recently voiced his dismay at the deteriorating morale he found prevalent at the Orange Glen station. Although his complaints were not laced with anger or threats, they were persistent for the few months preceding his crimes. He had also discussed with a number of coworkers the murders committed by another postal employee, Patrick Sherrill, in Edmond, Oklahoma. No one considered this particularly unusual since many employees were concerned about morale and safety throughout the U.S. Postal Service. There was no indication that John Taylor was preoccupied with the issue of deteriorating morale or that he was in any way obsessed with publicized incidents of workplace violence at the Postal Service.

Taylor had also expressed concern that postal inspectors were targeting him for investigation by planting cash along his postal route to see if he would keep the money. He always turned the cash over to postal authorities and was assured by them that it was all coincidence—he was under no scrutiny. A few of Taylor's coworkers claimed he always believed it was a secret investigation, and not coincidence, that made cash appear on his route so often. Again, there was no evidence indicating that Taylor was particularly upset by these circumstances or reacting in a particularly paranoid fashion. However, he was known to be a man who did not complain quickly or easily; probably, no one knew precisely how he felt about this or other matters that may have troubled him.

Finally there was the issue of drinking. Some of John Taylor's coworkers claimed he had a problem with alcohol but that he was able to keep it hidden from nearly everyone. In the end, no one knew if this was true or not since there was never any evidence to suggest any kind of dependency.

Since John Taylor had no negative history whatsoever, it is difficult to give full credence to statements made after his death that cast doubt on his character. The information provided by coworkers and neighbors after an incident such as this is always suspect. It would have been a natural reaction for those who knew Taylor to try to find some reason, no matter how insignificant, to help understand the murderous actions of an individual who was considered nonviolent throughout his entire life (see Table 2.8).

Still, one cannot discount the possibilities offered by those who knew John Taylor.

Analysis

The case of John Taylor is both troubling and important to an understanding of the lethal employee as his actions were virtually unpredictable to all who knew him. Taylor was a man who seemed settled, productive, honored in the workplace, and devoted to his family. Although there was some evidence of behavioral warning signs, these were not pervasive, long-standing, or severe. There appear to have been no triggering events linked to Taylor's crimes—at least none that have come to light. That those who knew John Taylor were shocked at his actions is completely understandable; there would have been no reason for anyone to expect him to harm another.

The key to understanding what caused John Taylor to become a lethal employee may lie in the murder of his wife. Unfortunately, no one knows why he killed the woman with whom he had spent so much of his life and who appeared to be the object of his devotion. Perhaps his marriage was not as strong as it appeared to be; perhaps there were other motivations known only to the Taylors. From the statements of those who knew the Taylors it is, at best, enigmatic that he would harm his wife.

Table 2.8: Summary of Characteristics: John M. Taylor

Male:	yes
Age range of 30-60 years:	yes
Evidence of social isolation:	no
Evidence of triggering events:	no
Vocalized violent intentions:	no
Exhibited behavior uncomfortable to coworkers:	no
History of violent behavior:	no
Evidence of psychosis or psychological disorder:	no
Evidence of obsession or delusional disorder:	no
Alcohol or chemical dependence:	possible
Severe or chronic depression:	no
Pathological blaming:	possible
Impaired neurological functioning:	no
Chronic or severe frustration:	possible
Preoccupation with weapons or paramilitary themes:	no
Evidence of severe personality disorder:	no

The questions raised by coworkers about Taylor's concern with office morale, postal investigations, or his possible abuse of alcohol, even if all true and accurate, do not present the picture of an employee driven to violence and murder. Even those who offered these possible motivating circumstances were quick to point out that John Taylor's reactions were typically reasonable and nonviolent. He never resorted to threats or intimidation and exhibited no discomforting behavior whatsoever. If any of these issues were linked to John Taylor's decision to murder, it is not apparent. The actions of John Taylor clearly emphasize what is *not* known about the lethal employee and what may never be known in some instances—his motivation. Although much has been learned about the lethal employee and efforts to predict and prevent violence are improving, there will always be incidents like the shootings at Orange Glen—crimes that speak to the unpredictability of the lethal employee and remind us that no predictive regimen can, in the end, be wholly reliable.

"I TOLD THEM I'D BE BACK"

The saga of "Rock" Wesbecker is, in many ways, a story of failed management. Wesbecker was a long-term employee with a good work record. Then it all went wrong for Wesbecker—his marriage failed and he became unable to handle the long-standing stresses inherent in his job. When he approached his employer for some relief, he was turned aside. Wesbecker's life went from bad to worse, and he went looking for revenge (see Table 2.9).

Table 2.9: Synopsis of Case Study No. 5

Perpetrator:	Joseph T. "Rock" Wesbecker
Age:	47
Family:	Divorced
Date of Incident:	September 14, 1989
Location of Incident:	Standard Gravure Corporation (Louisville, KT)
Employment Status:	Terminated after 20 years of service.
Work History:	Stable with good to excellent performance.
Criminal History:	None
Fatalities and Injuries:	8 killed, 15 injured
	Perpetrator committed suicide at the scene.

The Crime

Joseph Wesbecker, nicknamed "Rock", was a pressman for the Standard Gravure Corporation of Louisville, Kentucky. Wesbecker, however, was not just another pressman—he was one of the best the corporation had ever employed. After twenty years of service to the company, Joseph Wesbecker had earned his excellent reputation as a loyal and consistent employee; and he was obviously proud of it. His work was of such high quality that Wesbecker could command overtime pay practically whenever he chose—and he often did so. For nearly two decades, Joseph Wesbecker was a steadfast employee whose work was unquestioned. However, he was also a man with serious problems.

Joseph Wesbecker was suffering from significant job stress and a severe depression disorder. By 1987, Wesbecker's marriage had failed and the stress of his job, perhaps combined with the pressures brought on by so much overtime, had become intolerable. He approached corporate management for some relief, asking to be placed in a less stressful job, but he was denied. In that same year, having repeatedly failed in his attempts to find respite, Wesbecker filed a complaint against Standard Gravure with the Jefferson County Human Relations Commission, contending that the corporation was harassing him and not responding to his pleas for assistance. The corporation reacted by assigning Wesbecker to a noisy, high-speed press, despite the fact they were aware of his psychological condition and could reasonably assume he would be unable to cope with such a high-stress environment.[27] The following year, in an effort to settle the formal complaint against them, corporation executives agreed to place Wesbecker on long-term disability leave at 60 percent of his normal pay. They also agreed to reemploy Wesbecker when, and if, he recovered sufficiently to return to work.

Joseph Wesbecker was both ill and furious. He was out of work, completely disassociated from his sole source of social contact, abandoned by his employer of twenty years, and undergoing drug treatment for his depression. He was eventually placed on a regimen of Prozac to ease his deepening depression, a medication that has proven to be controversial due to the behavior-altering side effects it causes in some individuals. He was alone in his home, with nothing to divert his attention from his worsening condition, and his income cut in half. Joseph Wesbecker had little else to lose in his life; he was deeply angered at his circumstances and was convinced that the Standard Gravure Corporation was the progenitor of his problems.

Wesbecker purchased an AK-47 assault rife at a local gun shop in early 1989. Since before his layoff he had been vocalizing threats against the corporation and its management for the way he had been treated. He had frequently discussed other incidents of murder and workplace violence openly. Several months prior to his layoff, Wesbecker had confided in a coworker about his plans to bomb Standard Gravure or murder "a bunch of people" at the job site.[28] He had even discussed the idea with his ex-wife before they divorced and he found himself without a family or a job. At one point, Joseph Wesbecker considered hiring a professional assassin to murder certain company executives but abandoned the idea.[29] Clearly, Wesbecker was an angry man even prior to the loss of his job. Now he was alone, with little else to occupy his mind and completely absorbed in his growing anger and depression.

On September 13, 1989, the day before he returned to the Standard Gravure Corporation for the last time, Joseph Wesbecker cleaned and readied his firearms. Early the next morning, he left his personal effects on the kitchen table of his home (including a last will and testament), where they would be easily and quickly discovered. Filling a canvas bag with a variety of weapons and ammunition, and carrying the AK-47 he had purchased earlier that year, Joseph Wesbecker set out for the job site. Left behind on the table was a copy of *Time* magazine that featured an article about Patrick Purdy. Earlier that year, Purdy had murdered five children with an AK-47 at a Stockton, California, elementary school. The article was arranged so that the photograph of Purdy's AK-47 was face up on the kitchen table.[30] It was a weapon very similar to the one Joseph Wesbecker slung across his shoulder that morning as he left for the job site.

Wesbecker arrived at the company around 8:30 that morning. When he reached the plant, he immediately took the elevator to the third floor where the business and binding offices were located. Without speaking, he shot randomly throughout the office, working his way downstairs to a basement work area where he found more coworkers. Using both his AK-47 and a semiautomatic pistol he brought along, Wesbecker shot indiscriminately at his former colleagues. His rampage lasted for about twenty minutes, during which time he killed seven employees and wounded an additional fifteen. Witnesses at the scene claimed he fired at least forty rounds in an effort to annihilate those who crossed his path. In a final act of desperation, Joseph Wesbecker shot himself in the head, dying instantly at the scene.

The Perpetrator

Joseph Wesbecker overcame many difficulties in his life to become a successful and respected employee. When he was only a year old, Wesbecker's father died. At age four his grandfather, a person to whom Joseph had been deeply attached, also died. Throughout his younger years Wesbecker was moved from place to place and, at one point, was left in an orphanage for nearly a year. Understandably, given his difficult early years, Joseph was a poor student in school and dropped out in the ninth grade. From then until his tragic death, Wesbecker was a determined, extremely hard-working individual who valued his own efforts and ethics highly.

Joseph Wesbecker's life at home was always difficult. He was married and divorced twice, eventually becoming separated from nearly all family members. He was often alone and lonely. It was inevitable that Wesbecker's job would become the center of his life and the single point of self-esteem upon which he could rely and where he excelled. However, despite his reputation at work, Joseph Wesbecker was not a happy man (see Table 2.10).

In the workplace, Wesbecker gained a reputation as an extremely hard worker who persistently sought overtime hours to extend his income. Much of this extra pay allowed Wesbecker to invest in the stock market and, no doubt, was an important point of personal pride. His coworkers and supervisors universally regarded him as an excellent pressman whose quality of work and obvious dedication were beyond question. In the end, Joseph Wesbecker's job was the most important element in an otherwise stormy and lonely existence. It was not something he could give up easily.[31]

Joseph Wesbecker suffered from a serious depression disorder, and his supervisors at the corporation knew it. He was subject to periods of deep depression alternating with manic episodes. Individuals suffering from this debilitating disorder can, at times, exhibit almost no interest in ordinary daily activities, may suffer sleep disorders and fatigue, feel worthless or guilty, and suffer from a preoccupation with thoughts of death. During a manic episode the individual may react aggressively, exhibit inflated self-esteem, and demonstrate a vastly increased capacity for work or other activities. Wesbecker, who suffered significantly from this roller-coaster disorder, looked naturally to the organization for which he worked to provide relief and assistance. After all, he had given the company decades of loyal service, and he expected some consideration in return. In the end, however, the organization abandoned him, effectively denying him the last and most important element of self-esteem he had left. In retrospect, it cannot be too surprising that Joseph Wesbecker lashed out against this final disappointment in his life.

Analysis

The saga of Joseph Wesbecker and the Standard Gravure Corporation is a tragic one. There can be little doubt that the violence wrought by Wesbecker upon his fellow employees should have been foreseen and avoided. Over a significant period of time, Wesbecker exhibited many behavioral warning signs that can be seen, in retrospect, as classic. His obvious depression was known to company executives; his threats against the organization were known to his coworkers and his ex-wife. He had often telegraphed to others that he was a man in trouble, who was quickly reaching a point of desperation. Wesbecker made several attempts to get the help he needed by both approaching the management of the organization and pursuing a formal complaint. He repeatedly asked for assistance with his stress and depression; he was repeatedly denied or, in his opinion, harassed further for his efforts.

Table 2.10: Summary of Characteristics: Joseph T. Wesbecker

Male:	yes
Age range of 30-60 years:	yes
Evidence of social isolation:	yes
Evidence of triggering events:	yes
Vocalized violent intentions:	yes
Exhibited behavior uncomfortable to coworkers:	yes
History of violent behavior:	no
Evidence of psychosis or psychological disorder:	no
Evidence of obsession or delusional disorder:	no
Alcohol or chemical dependence:	no
Severe or chronic depression:	yes
Pathological blaming:	yes
Impaired neurological functioning:	no

From the evidence of the case history, there is no indication that Joseph Wesbecker refused any offers of assistance: quite the contrary, he repeatedly bargained for them. It is difficult to condone the actions of Joseph Wesbecker— too many innocent lives were lost. On the other hand, this incident should not have occurred. Wesbecker was a man who was deeply attached to his work and obviously loyal to his employer. His sole expectation was that his employer return this loyalty at a time when he was obviously in need. Certainly, this does not, on the face of it, seem to be an unreasonable expectation. Even though Joseph Wesbecker's actions were heinous and unforgivable, at a certain level they can be understood. They were, to a large extent, predictable.

The case of Joseph Wesbecker provides an uncomfortably stark representation of the importance of recognizing behavioral warning signs and acting on them. The management of the company could have shown a commitment to the wellness of a long-term employee and made efforts to assist him, with the eventual goal of returning him to the workplace as quickly as possible. There was every reason to believe that Joseph Wesbecker would be a loyal and efficient employee until the day he retired from Standard Gravure. The company could have demonstrated, to both Wesbecker and his coworkers, the high value they placed upon employees who were obviously committed to the organization. Instead, for whatever reason, they apparently abandoned him. Given the pervasive importance of his job, both economically and socially, this was something Joseph Wesbecker could not tolerate.

Beyond the questions raised within the case history, another possible contributing factor may have been at play in the actions of Joseph Wesbecker— his possible reactions to the antidepressant medication, Prozac. Survivors and family members of the victims of the tragedy at Standard Gravure Corporation brought suit against Eli Lilly, the manufacturer of Prozac, claiming that the drug triggered Joseph Wesbecker's deadly rampage. In all, well over 150 lawsuits have been filed against the drug manufacturer for a variety of reasons, generally centered around the contention that Prozac unexpectedly, and sometimes with devastation, altered the behavior of patients taking the medication. In December 1994, the jury hearing the case involving the crimes of Joseph Wesbecker rejected the lawsuit, finding no connection between the alleged effects of Prozac and Wesbecker's actions. Nonetheless, many questions still remain about the drug's alleged effects; the issue has not yet been resolved.

Despite this controversy, at the heart of this case history lies the obvious— Joseph Wesbecker exhibited multiple behavioral warning signs and made several attempts to get the help he knew he needed. The only remaining issue is why assistance was so painfully absent and why the obvious opportunities for positive intervention were ignored.

A HISTORY OF VIOLENCE

A history of violent behavior is arguably the most reliable predictor of future violence. An individual who demonstrates a pattern of reacting in a violent way is likely to repeat this behavior in the future. Many, if not most, of the violent individual's relationships are based upon the concepts of control and power—to stay in control or, if not, to achieve control by any means. Similarly, an individual who exhibits a strong defiance of authority, combined with a propensity for aggression, is likely to continue challenging and intimidating others in the future for the same reasons. Eventually, for this individual, life itself becomes a question of control and power—the basis for any relationship into which he or she ventures and the singular point to his or her behavior.

It is crucial to keep in mind that violent behavior often tends to escalate over time. A potentially violent individual may begin his life of aggression in small ways—with minor acts of defiance or by shouting and arguing with others. If this behavior continues and it goes unchecked, it is possible that he will escalate the level of violence until it becomes lethal. If the target of his aggression lies in the workplace, which is often the case with individuals who are violently defiant of authority, coworkers and supervisors are at significant risk. It may be just a matter of time before the angry, aggressive, violent individual becomes a lethal employee. This was the course of progressive violence that was apparent in the life of Thomas McIlvane—a man with a clear history of violence for most of his adult life (see Table 2.11).

Table 2.11: Synopsis of Case Study No. 6

Perpetrator:	Thomas McIlvane
Age:	31
Family:	Single
Date of Incident:	November 14, 1991
Location of Incident:	Royal Oak Post Office (MI)
Employment Status:	Terminated after 6 years of service.
Work History:	Erratic with frequent poor performance. A history of poor performance in the military.
Criminal History:	Insubordination in the military resulting in a less-than-honorable discharge; charged with making threats over the telephone when a civilian; involved in physical altercations and threats.
Fatalities and Injuries:	5 killed, 4 injured
	Perpetrator committed suicide at the scene.

The Crime

In 1990, the Royal Oak Post Office was assigned a new top management team. The U.S. General Accounting Office (GAO) had completed its audit of operations at the post office, and the news was not good. They had determined that employee-management relations at the station were strained and volatile. The GAO recommended changes in the management structure, and four new supervisors were assigned to the 160-employee Royal Oak station.

One of the Royal Oak employees about whom the new managers had been warned was Thomas McIlvane, a letter carrier with a five-year history of poor performance, violent outbursts, and general workplace disruption. An accomplished martial artist who was familiar with weapons, McIlvane had the reputation of a hothead who defied authority and was often physically aggressive; he would verbally threaten coworkers or supervisors and, when he felt it necessary, engage them in fights. However, McIlvane's new supervisor, Christopher Carlisle, was ready for the assignment and intent upon bringing some order to Royal Oak. He had come across troublemakers like McIlvane before, and his reputation as a strict disciplinarian was, in his mind, well earned. Other workers felt differently, however. Many employees viewed Carlisle as a man prone to administer by fear and intimidation—just the wrong type of supervisor for Thomas McIlvane.[32] A congressional investigation of the incident at Royal Oak would later say of Carlisle: "It is reported that Chris Carlisle would stand behind an employee and berate him or her hoping to provoke a response from the employee. If the employee then accosted Carlisle, he would discipline the employee."[33] Given McIlvane's notorious short fuse and Carlisle's intimidating style of management, it came as no surprise to the employees at Royal Oak that the two locked horns almost immediately.

On September 10, 1990, Thomas McIlvane was given a notice of intent to terminate his job for "gross insubordination."[34] This notice provided him with the right for arbitration and, if he won, reinstatement. While waiting for the arbitration hearing, McIlvane would be placed on unpaid leave. McIlvane knew it could be a long time before he would appear before the arbitrator to plead his case. Carlisle also knew this and probably felt it was a good way to get McIlvane out of the workforce—at least for a while.

McIlvane's arbitration hearing was delayed for over a year—an absurdly long period of time to allow such a serious matter to remain unresolved. During those many months, Thomas McIlvane made repeated threats against Carlisle and other supervisors at the station. He even threatened the director of field operations by telephone, saying: "Fuck you, faggot postmaster. I'm going to be watching you, and I'm going to get you."[35] A number of other post office employees reported similar threats from McIlvane, as did a number of union officials helping him with his appeal. One union official later stated that McIlvane said, "If I lose the arbitration, it will make Edmond, Oklahoma, look like a tea party." He was referring to the incident in 1986 when Patrick Sherrill, a letter carrier like McIlvane, murdered fourteen, injured six, and killed himself in a rampage at the Edmond, Oklahoma, Post Office.

McIlvane finally had his appeal on November 12, 1991. It was everything Carlisle had expected. Later that day, after the hearing, McIlvane learned that his termination had been sustained by the arbitrator—the news was left on his home answering machine.[36] McIlvane was, predictably, furious and out of options. He now had little left to lose and had developed a monumental grudge against his supervisors and everyone else at Royal Oak. On November 14, two days after the hearing, McIlvane armed himself with a .22-caliber semiautomatic rifle and hundreds of rounds of ammunition. Just before 9:00 in the morning, he arrived at the Royal Oak Post Office for the final time.

McIlvane slipped through an unlocked door used by post office employees. The rifle, which had been sawed off, was hidden beneath his clothes. He quickly sought out his primary target, Christopher Carlisle, whom he killed instantly with a powerful blast from his weapon. At the first sound of gunfire, post office employees began to scatter, prompting McIlvane to begin firing at random.

At the end of his rampage, McIlvane had murdered four people and seriously injured another four—a terrible toll, but one that could have been much worse had the employees in the area not scattered as quickly as they did.

McIlvane's final act of retribution was to raise the rifle to his own head and pull the trigger, dying instantly a few feet from his first victim.

The Perpetrator

Thomas McIlvane was an angry man throughout his adult life (see Table 2.12). Even before joining the postal service, when he was a marine, McIlvane's propensity for aggression was nearly legend. While serving in the military, he had been demoted in rank several times for refusing to carry out orders and because of his aggressive, violent behavior. After several such incidents, he was discharged from the marines without honors, making him ineligible to serve in the reserves—something he had wanted to do. Despite the nature of his discharge, McIlvane received a veteran's preference points benefit for any civil service job. This advantage led to his employment at the Royal Oak Post Office.[37]

Joining the postal service did nothing for Thomas McIlvane's disposition; he was in trouble almost from the first day he started work. McIlvane received numerous warnings for unauthorized leave from the job, not following his preassigned postal route, fighting with customers, and arguing with supervisors. He was by far the most troublesome employee at Royal Oak.

McIlvane responded to each disciplinary action with increased anger and escalating threats. He was locked into a struggle for control and power with everyone he knew. Virtually all his coworkers were aware of McIlvane's numerous threats against his supervisors, themselves, and even customers; most were justifiably afraid of him. As McIlvane's behavior became more unstable and violent, he was eventually charged with making threatening telephone calls and stood trial for the offense. However, he was acquitted for lack of evidence. Some six months before his rampage, in May 1991, the local police revoked McIlvane's permit to carry a concealed weapon because they had received so many complaints about his threatening behavior.

Thomas McIlvane had, for years, telegraphed to all he knew that he was a violent man with few limits on his behavior. When interviewed by the press after the murders, few of his coworkers expressed surprise at what had occurred. Many claimed they had expected McIlvane to do something violent— perhaps even resort to murder. Most who knew him were afraid of his unpredictable temper and avoided him in any way they could. Although numerous Royal Oak employees said they had filed complaints about McIlvane's behavior, apparently none of these were investigated. The response of the GAO to the deteriorating situation at Royal Oak—by sending in a new team of supervisors—did not address the long-standing feelings of anger harbored by Thomas McIlvane. Indeed, it may have escalated a situation, which was apparently already out of control, toward an immediate and lethal finale.

Table 2.12: Summary of Characteristics: Thomas McIlvane

Male:	yes
Age range of 30-60 years:	yes
Evidence of social isolation:	yes
Evidence of triggering events:	yes
Vocalized violent intentions:	yes
Exhibited behavior uncomfortable to coworkers:	yes
History of violent behavior:	yes
Evidence of psychosis or psychological disorder:	no
Evidence of obsession or delusional disorder:	no
Alcohol or chemical dependence:	no
Severe or chronic depression:	no
Pathological blaming:	yes
Impaired neurological functioning:	no
Chronic or severe frustration:	yes
Preoccupation with weapons or paramilitary themes:	yes
Evidence of severe personality disorder:	possible

Analysis

The most shocking element surrounding the murders committed by Thomas McIlvane was that they were almost expected by many of his coworkers. So frequent were his outbursts and so clear his intentions that those who knew him *expected* him to react violently. Their reactions were instinctive—to avoid dealing with McIlvane at any cost. Unfortunately, these reactions helped perpetuate his propensity for violence. Because the management at Royal Oak permitted McIlvane to behave erratically for years without undertaking positive and effective intervention to diffuse his aggression, they enabled him to take the course he chose. These murders might have been prevented had McIlvane's supervisors been trained in techniques of intervention and prevention—had they not, in the end, resorted to the tactics of force favored by McIlvane himself.

For years, Thomas McIlvane had made obvious his delight in using tactics of intimidation and aggression. His pervasive defiance of authority was legend. Any reasonable investigation into McIlvane's background, despite the issue of the veteran's preference points, would surely pinpoint him as a potentially violent employee. Any reasonable efforts to investigate and take action on the many complaints from his coworkers about McIlvane's behavior could have potentially prevented the killings. There must have been many opportunities to intervene, but none were apparently exploited.

The final triggering event—advising McIlvane of his ultimate termination by a recorded message—proved to be the last in a number of classic management failures that virtually guaranteed a murderous outcome by a man who had often said he would get even and clearly meant it.

DRUG ABUSE

The story of Robert Mack is a tragic one. Mack worked for a major corporation all his life and was well regarded by his supervisors. He was financially secure, owned his own home, and enjoyed the companionship of a spouse and three children. However, as bright as the future seemed to be for Robert Mack, it all went terribly wrong. He lost his wife and children, became severely addicted to cocaine, and was eventually fired from his job. Out of options and out of control, Mack, who had never exhibited any indication of violence, became a classic lethal employee (see Table 2.13).

Table 2.13: Synopsis of Case Study No. 7

Perpetrator:	Robert E. Mack
Age:	42
Family:	Separated from his wife and three children.
Date of Incident:	January 24, 1992
Location of Incident:	General Dynamics Corporation (San Diego, CA)
Employment Status:	Employed at General Dynamics for 25 years. Terminated from the company nine days before the incident.
Work History:	Satisfactory until the year before his termination.
Criminal History:	None
Fatalities and Injuries:	1 killed, 1 injured
	Perpetrator survived. Sentenced to life imprisonment for murder and 15 years to life for attempted murder.

The Crime

Robert Mack joined General Dynamics Corporation when he dropped out of high school at the age of seventeen. By the beginning of 1992, Mack had worked for the company for twenty-five years, earned a top-secret security clearance, and held the position of production distribution analyst. His primary responsibility was to track missing documents related to cruise missile production so that security for the project would not be compromised.[38] It was a responsible job, and one that had been awarded to Robert Mack because of his many years of loyal and reliable service. He was reliable, that is, until 1991— the year he became addicted to cocaine.

About a year before he was fired from his job, Mack began to show up late for work. His occasional tardiness grew worse and eventually became flagrant. By the beginning of 1992, Robert Mack was late more often than he was on time, had a history of unexcused absences, and had been counseled numerous times by his supervisor. He was also struggling financially because of the unmanageable expense of his cocaine habit. Although he never argued when counseled and had no history of threatening his supervisor, repeated attempts to encourage Mack to straighten up and return to his two-decade history of good performance and reliability failed. After having exhausted all attempts to get Mack's cooperation, the corporation decided that the situation was not salvageable. On January 15, 1992, Robert Mack was terminated from his job and lifelong career.

A hearing was scheduled for January 24, 1992, to allow Mack and his union representatives to present their case and ask management to reconsider their decision. The meeting was scheduled for 1:00 in the afternoon, but Robert Mack, as had become his trademark, was forty minutes late.[39] Waiting for his arrival was Mack's former supervisor and the labor negotiator for General Dynamics. Three union representatives were also at the meeting to advocate for Mack's reinstatement. When Mack finally arrived, none of the five individuals present in the conference room noticed anything unusual about his behavior— he was as quiet and passive as he had always been, but perhaps a bit more withdrawn than usual. No one at the meeting was aware that Robert Mack had managed to enter the premises with a handgun concealed on his person.

The hearing broke up after less than an hour with the parties agreeing that progress had been made. A second hearing was scheduled for the following week, and the union representatives agreed that the meeting had gone well; Robert Mack's chances for reinstatement had improved. As the attendees left the conference room, Mack lingered behind in the chair he had quietly occupied throughout the meeting. His former supervisor and the labor negotiator walked out into the nearby courtyard where about two dozen other employees were taking an afternoon break, gathering in small conversational groups.

Just after the two executives entered the courtyard, Robert Mack stepped away from his chair and trailed after them. Without speaking a word, Mack pulled out a .38-caliber handgun, which had been concealed under his clothing, and, in quick succession, shot both men in the head. One of the executives died instantly, the other recovered after a long struggle.

Still carrying the weapon at his side, Mack walked slowly from the courtyard, looking for a telephone and speaking to no one along his way. Coworkers immediately called for emergency police assistance, which arrived in only a few moments. Officers began to surround the premises and search for the shooter, whom many employees had already recognized.

After several minutes of wandering the corridors, Mack was able to find a telephone and placed a call to his mother at her residence. After hearing her voice, Mack dictated very specific instructions about his funeral arrangements, even specifying the music that should be played at the service. He explained to his frightened mother that he intended to end his life there and then and wanted her assurances that his funeral arrangements would be just as he wanted. After holding a long and rambling conversation with his mother, while surrounded by numerous law enforcement officers with their guns drawn, Mack changed his mind about suicide and quietly surrendered to the waiting authorities.

Robert Mack was charged with one count of murder and one count of attempted murder. Because he was financially destitute, Mack was appointed a public defender; he pled not guilty by reason of insanity. His trial was not a long one and eventually ended in a hung jury; although agreeing that he was guilty, the jurors were unable to determine Mack's *degree* of culpability and became hopelessly deadlocked. A second trial was ordered but, on the day it was to begin, Robert Mack surprised the court by pleading guilty to both counts. He was sentenced to a life term on the murder charge and a second term of fifteen years to life on the charge of attempted murder, with the terms to run consecutively. Under the sentence imposed by the court, Robert Mack would become eligible for parole after seventeen years.

The Perpetrator

Robert Mack had no criminal record or history of violence before his murderous outburst in 1992. He worked for General Dynamics exclusively for his entire adult life and was a trusted employee with a high security clearance. After his arrest, Mack said this about his job: "I enjoyed my job. I loved my job. That's all I lived for, was to go to work and come home."[40] For twenty-four of his twenty-five years on the job, it was clear that Mack was a reliable worker with a good performance record. Moreover, it was evident to all who knew him that Mack was quite happy at General Dynamics. However, despite his solid reputation at work and the pleasure he took in his job, not all was well with Robert Mack (see Table 2.14).

In 1977, Robert Mack's marriage failed and his wife and three children left him. He remained, alone, in the house they had occupied together since 1969. Mack had always been socially withdrawn and never involved himself in neighborhood or community activities. After the separation from his family, however, Mack's isolation became both chronic and severe. He was rarely seen by his neighbors, had no friends, and relied exclusively on his job for any social interaction.

Approximately twelve months before he was fired from his job, Mack began to use cocaine. His addiction became severe, and he suffered a series of financial setbacks by attempting to keep up with his habit. Mack's performance at work began to deteriorate rapidly and significantly. Within a year of beginning his drug use, Robert Mack was unable to function on the job. His tardiness was legendary, his absences from work were extreme, and all efforts by his employer to intervene were unsuccessful. By the time Mack committed his crime, he claimed to suffer periods of delusion, hallucinations, and blackouts. At his trial, Mack said he was completely unaware of many of the events surrounding his activities on January 24, 1992.

Table 2.14: Summary of Characteristics: Robert E. Mack

Male:	yes
Age range of 30-60 years:	yes
Evidence of social isolation:	yes
Evidence of triggering events:	yes
Vocalized violent intentions:	no
Exhibited behavior uncomfortable to coworkers:	no
History of violent behavior:	no
Evidence of psychosis or psychological disorder:	no
Evidence of obsession or delusional disorder:	no
Alcohol or chemical dependence:	yes
Severe or chronic depression:	no
Pathological blaming:	no
Impaired neurological functioning:	no
Chronic or severe frustration:	no
Preoccupation with weapons or paramilitary themes:	no
Evidence of severe personality disorder:	no

Analysis

It is clear that Robert Mack suffered from a severe addiction to cocaine, which probably played a large part in his violent outburst at General Dynamics. Moreover, he suffered a major triggering event in losing his job which, by his own admission, had become the sole purpose of his life. When Mack's home was examined by police officials after the shooting, they discovered a vast number of work-related manuals and company reading materials dating back to the time he was first employed by General Dynamics. It was evident that when Mack declared that his job was crucial to his life he was not overstating his sentiments.

Robert Mack was significantly socially isolated, having separated from his family some fifteen years before he lost his job. He had no friends and did not interact with neighbors. As the years passed and Mack became involved with the use of cocaine, he was rarely seen outside his home and apparently had no social network on which to rely in a time of crisis. With the final triggering event of losing his job, while suffering from a severe drug addiction, Mack was out of control and, in his mind, out of options. Despite the willingness of his employer to intervene and even reconsider their decision to terminate his employment, Robert Mack was beyond help and unable to respond with anything but revenge. His crimes are a vivid example of the pernicious effects brought on by drug abuse and addiction.

ALL THE WARNING SIGNS

The murders committed by Dr. Valery Fabrikant are among the best analyzed in the literature because of the venue in which they were carried out—the campus of a major university. Fabrikant often displayed classic behavioral warning signs indicating potential violence. In fact, virtually everyone who worked with Fabrikant came to the realization that he was an obvious threat to others in the workplace. Despite the warning signs and general knowledge of the man's growing aggression, however, he was able to carry out his revenge without intervention from the university (see Table 2.15).

The Crime

Dr. Valery Fabrikant first arrived at Concordia University in December 1979. He was a Russian émigré who possessed a U.S. "green card" and was traveling on Italian papers.[41] Fabrikant was unknown to anyone at the university but insisted upon meeting personally with the chair of the Department of Mechanical Engineering about a job. He presented himself as a scientist and educator of significant standing in Russia. Although it was not the practice of the university, or the chair, to interview applicants without established appointments and background information, Fabrikant's persistence in returning each day until he was interviewed paid off. He was able to meet with the chair of the department and receive, on the spot, a job offer as a research assistant to begin immediately. His first day of employment was December 20, 1979.

By 1982, Dr. Fabrikant had been promoted to research assistant professor and was teaching a class in probability and statistics. This promotion should have been accompanied by three letters of reference and additional background information. However, in the case of Fabrikant, this requirement was never fulfilled. University officials knew nothing of Fabrikant before he arrived at Concordia, but they were quickly learning, even at this early stage of their relationship, that any "interaction with him was fraught with sharp edges."[42] In less than three years, Valery Fabrikant had established himself as a difficult, argumentative, and unpredictable individual—and one who seemed to set no limits on his own behavior. In that same year, a female student complained to university officials that she had been raped by Fabrikant. The victim was so distraught and in such fear that she begged the ombudsperson with whom she spoke to not allow the information to go any further. She had been injured sufficiently in the attack that she had a police officer take her to a hospital, where it was determined she had suffered a dislocated shoulder. A police report was subsequently filed, but no further action was taken. The ombudsperson, who was clearly in a difficult position, elected to keep the matter confidential, feeling that if knowledge of the crime was made public, the victim would be put in even greater jeopardy.

Table 2.15: Synopsis of Case Study No. 8

Perpetrator:	Valery Fabrikant
Age:	53
Family:	Single
Date of Incident:	August 24, 1992
Location of Incident:	On the campus of Concordia University (Quebec, Montreal, Canada).
Employment Status:	Employed at Concordia University for 13 years.
Work History:	Apparently satisfactory in Canada (unknown in Russia).
Criminal History:	None in Canada, unknown in Russia.
Fatalities and Injuries:	4 killed, 1 injured
	Perpetrator survived. Sentenced to life imprisonment in 1993.

By 1983, Fabrikant was openly argumentative and hostile with most coworkers and intimidating to many students. He was banned several times from certain classes because of his behavior and his propensity to harass and intimidate the instructors. By 1988, his reputation as being hostile, aggressive, and unpredictable had become legendary on campus. Even the Purchasing Services Department of the university refused to do business with him. Administrators at Concordia held private meetings to discuss Fabrikant's obvious and unsettling behavioral problems but did nothing to change his course. By 1989, his tenth year at Concordia, Dr. Fabrikant was complaining persistently about how poorly he had been treated by the university and that he had been victimized by other professors, who had stolen his research work to incorporate into their own publications. He also began to vocalize clear threats of violence such as, "I know how people get what they want, they shoot a lot of people."[43] Dr. Fabrikant also made threats against the rector of the university, which she took so seriously that she ordered personal security protection. In response to the escalating threat that Fabrikant presented to the institution, several administrators consulted an outside psychiatrist about how to handle his behavior. Ironically, throughout this period, Fabrikant received regular merit salary increases and academic recognition, yet nothing was done to thwart the menace presented by his erratic behavior.

By the end of 1990, Fabrikant was accorded the position of associate professor on a two-year probationary status. Attached to this offer were no conditions that addressed Fabrikant's aggressive and hostile behavior throughout the university.   Within a year of his appointment, Fabrikant embarked on a vicious campaign of words against a number of individuals within the ranks of the university. Many of Fabrikant's complaints centered around his perception of the lack of ethics among his coworkers and the university in general. Although some of his points were meritorious, many were not; some were even bizarre. Fabrikant's attacks often included threats, personal humiliation, and extreme sarcasm. His aggressive behavior among his peers also intensified to such an extent that some of his colleagues had panic buttons installed on their desks or additional deadbolts affixed to their office doors as a precaution. It was clear to many at the university that Fabrikant's behavior was out of control.

Beginning with the new year in 1992, Fabrikant escalated his verbal assaults, some of which contained strange and disjointed accusations. According to Dr. John S. Cowan, the author of an extensive report dealing with Fabrikant's employment at Concordia University, "Throughout this period Dr. Fabrikant was widening the war, writing to all and sundry outside the University about his grievances, real and imagined."[44] At least one university administrator expressed deep concern about meeting with Fabrikant personally, regardless of the issues at hand. By May of that year, "there was evidence that Dr. Fabrikant's wars had nearly totally distracted him from his science."[45] In June, Fabrikant petitioned university administrators to allow him to carry a handgun on campus. His request was forcefully turned down three weeks later. University administrators were now gravely concerned about Fabrikant's behavior and again consulted an outside psychiatrist as well as legal counsel. They were clearly searching for a way out of a quickly deteriorating situation.

Fabrikant continued his aggressive tactics electronically, using e-mail and public discussion forums on the Internet. He was particularly obsessed with the ideation—paranoid or not—that several coworkers were stealing his original research and benefiting unfairly from its publication. A week before he murdered his colleagues, Dr. Fabrikant wrote, in part, the following:

I raise [the] question of "scientific prostitution." The main difference between scientific prostitution and "honorary authorship" is that in the first case a completely bogus scientist, not capable of doing any research, hires somebody from developing countries or [the] USSR by using [a] governmental grant. This someone does research in which the parasite supervisor is included as author. The more publications this parasite accumulates, the greater grant he gets, the more people he can hire, the more publications he gets, etc.[46]

Fabrikant continued the message by naming two colleagues whom he considered "parasites." He then filed suit against the two researchers, claiming they had demanded he name them as coauthors of various journal articles when, in fact, they had nothing at all to do with his research. This communication from Fabrikant, combined with numerous others that he publicly released on the Internet, resulted in a spate of suits against the embattled professor.

Finally the university administrators had had enough. Dr. Fabrikant was warned, in strong terms, that he must immediately stop his erratic behavior and desist from his outrageous verbal attacks on others. However, the warnings only served to fuel his growing hostility:

By August, Dr. Fabrikant was in trouble on a number of fronts. He risked contempt of court for his comments about Mr. Justice Gold contained in his vituperative e-mail messages, he faced a most taxing shift in teaching in the fall, he was facing lawsuits, and launching others, and had utterly alienated even CUFA, his faculty association. His big e-mail campaign to vilify his enemies was beginning to backfire. But he still had full access to the campus and its facilities.[47]

On August 24, 1992, Fabrikant came to Concordia University's Hall Building seeking revenge. Armed with three handguns and a briefcase filled with ammunition, he made his way to the ninth floor, where his own offices, and those of other colleagues, were located. Fabrikant first entered the office of a fifty-three-year-old biochemist whom he shot point-blank in the head. He then moved to an adjoining office, where he fatally shot a professor of mechanical engineering. Leaving the office, near the doorway, he shot a sixty-six-year-old department secretary who happened to be in the wrong place at the wrong time. Avoiding a chaotic rush of students who had heard the shooting, Fabrikant moved down the hallway, entered the office of the chairman of the electrical and engineering department, and shot him in the stomach. He then noticed a fellow professor who had rushed toward the sound of his gunfire; Fabrikant shot him twice in the head, killing him instantly.[48] At the end of his rampage, two coworkers had been killed at the scene and two others mortally wounded; a student was temporarily taken hostage, and a fifth coworker was wounded, but survived. After negotiating with law enforcement officials for some ninety minutes, Fabrikant was taken into custody without further injuries.

Fabrikant went on trial in 1993 after two court-appointed psychiatrists determined that he was sane but severely hostile and paranoid. During the course of his trial, Dr. Fabrikant received six contempt-of-court citations and hired—then fired—ten lawyers. At the end of the trial he was acting as his own attorney, making the case that his actions were provoked by coworkers at the university.

At the conclusion of the trial, Fabrikant was found guilty of four counts of murder; he was sentenced to the maximum penalty under Canadian law—life imprisonment.

The Perpetrator

Little objective information is available about Valery Fabrikant before he arrived in Canada at the approximate age of forty. His history at Concordia University is, however, known and has been documented. By most accounts, Fabrikant was considered a man of high intellect, an innovative researcher, and an effective instructor. There is little dispute that he was an impressive scientist in his own right. There were, however, many questions raised about the depth and veracity of his experience in Russia. In fact, the validity of Fabrikant's curriculum vitae (CV) was seriously questioned by several of his colleagues. In fairness to the professor, these discrepancies may have resulted from his developing understanding of a new language and equivalent responsibilities in Canada as contrasted to his native Russia.

From both his scientific contributions on campus and his writing, it seems obvious that the professor was academically qualified for his position. However, he was also extremely erratic and unpredictable in his behavior, apparently favoring aggressive tactics with most colleagues. The professor's reputation among his students was not as extreme; many believed him to be a first-rate instructor who was more than willing to help them understand difficult concepts.

It would be easy to characterize Valery Fabrikant as simply an erratic academic or a researcher with bizarre behavioral patterns; as a solitary, middle-aged professor who considered little else but his science. In fact, many of his colleagues may have held just this perception according to Dr. Cowan's observations. In reality, however, it appears that Fabrikant was a far more complex individual (see Table 2.16). His actions indicate that he was very aware of serious issues beyond his science, well aware of the power structure of the university, willing to aggressively challenge others on virtually any subject, and painfully sensitive to matters of ethics and honesty when his research efforts were involved. The professor apparently had an interest in a wide array of issues, but he was not often prone to listen to others if they held differing opinions of the issue at hand.

One must consider the possibility of cultural displacement, which may have contributed to Fabrikant's actions. The professor made it clear that he felt victimized by his colleagues, in part, on the grounds that he was from Russia and was therefore perpetually struggling with a new environment and a very different, Western code of ethics. He arrived in the West alone and was compelled to integrate into a complex, competitive environment with little or no support from others. No doubt he was viewed as a threat by more than one colleague at the university; it would be interesting to learn what, if any, support he received from colleagues who were not threatened by the new and obviously bright addition to their ranks. One cannot discount the possibility that this cultural displacement may have exacerbated the many frustrations experienced by the professor and, in the end, contributed to his violent outburst. This is an issue that is only open to speculation, not facts; nonetheless, it may be of importance in understanding the actions of Fabrikant and other individuals facing similar circumstances.

Much will never be known about Valery Fabrikant unless he someday chooses to divulge verifiable personal information. It would benefit others, and perhaps the professor himself, if more could be learned about him, his motivations, and his background. Until then, much of what motivated Dr. Fabrikant's actions at Concordia University must remain speculative.

Table 2.16: Summary of Characteristics: Valery Fabrikant

Male:	yes
Age range of 30-60 years:	yes
Evidence of social isolation:	yes
Evidence of triggering events:	uncertain
Vocalized violent intentions:	yes
Exhibited behavior uncomfortable to coworkers:	yes
History of violent behavior:	yes
Evidence of psychosis or psychological disorder:	uncertain
Evidence of obsession or delusional disorder:	no
Alcohol or chemical dependence:	no
Severe or chronic depression:	no
Pathological blaming:	yes
Impaired neurological functioning:	no
Chronic or severe frustration:	yes
Preoccupation with weapons or paramilitary themes:	no
Evidence of severe personality disorder:	uncertain

Analysis

In late 1993, after Fabrikant had been tried and sentenced, the board of governors at Concordia University ordered an independent review of certain aspects of the events leading up to the murders in 1992. Special emphasis was to be given to Fabrikant's employment history and the interactions between him and key members of the university hierarchy. In November 1993, the executive committee of the board appointed Dr. John S. Cowan from the University of Ottawa to undertake this task. He was given six months in which to produce a final report.

When Cowan presented his findings to the board of governors at Concordia University in May 1994, he included a detailed history of the thirteen year relationship between Fabrikant and the university. In addition, Cowan offered many astute observations about Fabrikant himself as well as about the actions taken by administrators at the university in their efforts to cope with the difficulties he presented in the workplace. One of these observations was based on Cowan's analysis of numerous pieces of correspondence written by Fabrikant on a variety of subjects. Cowan noticed that something was obviously absent in all Fabrikant's communications with others:

What is missing is any indication that Dr. Fabrikant ever feels or expresses any compassion about, concern for, or even interest in the well-being (or existence, for that matter) of any other adult human being.

This is the disconnectedness which deeply alarmed some, who certainly sensed at a visceral level that they were dealing with a person without limits on behavior, while others with more conventional antennae passed him off as merely another insensitive, self-centered ivory tower researcher, of which there are always a few in any large group of scholars.[49]

If this observation sounds familiar within the context of certain behavioral warning signs of the potentially lethal employee, it is because Cowan's assessment closely parallels key behavioral features exhibited by an individual suffering from borderline personality disorder or antisocial personality disorder. Indicators such as (1) a disregard for the rights of others, (2) a pathological fear of rejection (abandonment), and (3) indifference to others are prevalent in these disorders. In addition, as evidenced from the facts of this case history, there are other indicators clearly exhibited by Dr. Fabrikant, such as (1) repeated nonconformance to regulations and social norms, (2) impulsive and erratic behavior, (3) irritability and aggressiveness, and (4) a lack of remorse for the implications of his actions.

Obviously, it is not wise to assume the presence of either disorder in Fabrikant; this form of speculation is often incorrect and misleading. The best evidence available about his psychological state was that offered by the court-appointed psychiatrists, who found the professor hostile, aggressive, and paranoid. Fabrikant also displayed a pattern of verbal behavior which could be characterized as violent. He was socially isolated and without a significant relationship in his life, engaged in pathological blaming of others, and appeared to exhibit a chronic level of frustration. In short, the professor matched most of the personal characteristics and exhibited several behavioral characteristics of the potentially lethal employee.

It is not clear if there was a specific triggering event that prompted Dr. Fabrikant's rampage on August 24, 1992. It is evident that the professor was deeply engaged on all fronts with issues of ethics and the law. He was obviously and severely embattled as a result of his continuing aggression and his verbal attacks against colleagues. Whether a specific incident in this foray of words—which escalated so significantly the month before the shootings—triggered his actions is not known. It was Fabrikant's unshakable belief, as he made clear during the trial, that he felt compelled to aggression because of the actions of his colleagues. The professor's belief that several of his colleagues were benefiting unfairly from his original research may have had merit. What is not understandable, however, is why he felt compelled to settle this grievance in such an extreme manner.

THIS IS WHAT YOU ALL GET

Paul Calden was an angry man who let everyone around him know it. Living in near-complete isolation, his life centered around the workplace. This was also the center of his social network—one he liked to dominate by threats and intimidation. His behavior was so threatening and disruptive that one of his employers chose to offer him an exceptionally generous severance package just to leave the organization. However, Calden's next employer was not so fortunate. When Paul Calden was terminated from his last job, he promised to return to settle the score, and he did so with a vengeance.

The Crime

On January 27, 1993, Paul Calden returned to the offices of Fireman's Fund Insurance Company for the first time since he was terminated in March of the prior year (see Table 2.17). Hired by the company in 1990, Calden's stay with Fireman's Fund had been a short two years. At the time he was fired for misconduct and threatening a supervisor, Calden made it clear to coworkers that he would be back to get even with those whom he perceived as responsible for the loss of his job. Many of Calden's coworkers considered this threat more than idle, and with good reason.

Calden, a former claims manager at Fireman's Fund, was dressed in a dark blue business suit the day he returned for revenge. He had tried to disguise himself by wearing dark sunglasses and changing his hairstyle, but the attempt was only half-hearted; after all, the numbers were in his favor. Fireman's Fund was home to some 250 employees and, during the lunch hour, the crowds in the common areas, like the ground-floor eatery, would make him less obvious to those who knew his reputation as a man who was aggressive, hostile, and quick to anger.

When he arrived at the Tampa complex at noon that day, Calden went directly to the cafeteria of the office building, presuming he would find the targets of his revenge lunching together, as they often did. He had planned his actions out carefully, knowing where and when he would be able to attack with maximum devastation. At least one of Calden's former coworkers *did* recognize him as he entered the cafeteria but did not warn any of his coworkers. The man wondered why Calden was there—his recollection of Calden as a troublemaker was still strong and disturbing—but he concluded that the former employee may have found a new job in the office building, which housed several organizations in addition to Fireman's Fund.

Calden ordered lunch at the cafeteria counter and sat at a table by himself, waiting. For more than an hour he worked away at his lunch, sipped on a soft drink, and paced from the cafeteria to the adjoining patio, waiting for his victims to arrive. Eventually, they came. Calden's former supervisor, accompanied by key members of the company's management team, arrived together just after one o'clock. They ordered lunch and sat at a table near the back of the cafeteria, just as he knew they would.

Once they had settled in for their meal, Paul Calden was ready to strike. He moved quickly toward their table, appearing to work his way toward a trash container to dispose of an empty soda can. Instead, now next to their table, Calden pulled a .9-millimeter semiautomatic handgun from inside his suit jacket, yelling, "This is what you all get for firing me!" as he began shooting. In a cool, almost mechanical way, Calden circled the table, placing the barrel of his handgun at the head of each victim in turn and squeezing the trigger. Within thirty seconds he had fired off at least ten rounds, killing three of his former colleagues and seriously wounding another two. One of the shots shattered a large glass window in the cafeteria, sending shards hurtling throughout the area. Hearing the shots and breaking glass, employees dived for cover or made a rush for the exit in desperate attempts to stay alive. The scene was one of chaos, except for Paul Calden. He knew precisely who he wanted to kill and kept to his list of victims. For example, Calden deliberately bypassed one of the women sitting at the table, who survived the ordeal uninjured; she had played no part in his termination the previous year.

Table 2.17: Synopsis of Case Study No. 9

Perpetrator:	Paul Calden
Age:	33
Family:	Single
Date of Incident:	January 27, 1993
Location of Incident:	Restaurant in a building occupied by Fireman's Fund Insurance Company (Tampa, FL).
Employment Status:	Terminated 10 months prior to the incident.
Work History:	Employed at Fireman's Fund for 2 years with a questionable work history.
Criminal History:	None
Fatalities and Injuries:	3 killed, 2 injured
	Perpetrator committed suicide on a nearby golf course.

When he was finished with his rampage, Calden had slain the corporate controller, the operations manager, and a vice president of Fireman's Fund, while seriously wounding the human resources manager and a senior underwriter who was also at the table. Calden had nearly wiped out the senior management of the company in under a minute. He had exacted his revenge against those who had fired him—just as he had promised he would.

Apparently undisturbed by the chaos around him, Paul Calden quietly left the cafeteria by the front exit, depositing his gun next to the cash register on his way out. He then drove a late-model car, which he had rented especially for this day, some fifteen miles to a golf course in nearby Clearwater. Once there, Calden casually strolled to the thirteenth hole of the golf course and sat underneath a tree. In this serene environment, he produced another weapon—this time a .357-magnum revolver—from inside his jacket, fatally shooting himself in the head. When interviewed after the incident about why Paul

Calden had selected this place to commit suicide, the local golf pro could only add: "Nobody knows why he picked that hole. Obviously he laid himself to rest where he felt most at peace."[50]

The Perpetrator

Paul Calden was a good student in high school and college. He attended the University of Florida, where he easily graduated in four years, apparently on his way to a successful career in business. However, after graduation, things went wrong for Calden. He never managed to fit into the business community and never developed a meaningful social life. In fact, he had trouble with every job he held, jumping from employer to employer, seemingly on a regular schedule. His reputation in the workplace was one of a troublemaker; that of a man who was hostile, aggressive, and fond of threatening his coworkers.

Prior to joining Fireman's Fund in 1990, Calden worked for the Allstate Insurance Company. This was another of his relatively short-lived jobs. His reputation at Allstate was very bad. He threatened coworkers and frequently disrupted the work environment. Supervisors and colleagues considered Calden unstable and worrisome. He had a habit of bringing a handgun to work in a briefcase and displaying the butt of the gun to those he wanted to intimidate, taking obvious pleasure in their frightened reactions. Eventually he did this to a senior manager of the company, prodding the organization to take action. The management of Allstate agreed to offer Paul Calden a generous severance package and a positive written recommendation if he agreed to quit his job—they were that desperate to be rid of him; that afraid of what he might do next. Calden accepted Allstate's offer, pocketed his substantial severance benefits, and left the company.

The written recommendation provided by Allstate was Calden's ticket to his new job as a claims manager at Fireman's Fund. After the murders of January 1993, this recommendation would also lie at the core of a lawsuit brought against Allstate by the relatives and survivors of Paul Calden's actions. Their contention was a good one—how could an organization like Allstate provide a positive recommendation to an employee who they knew was unstable, aggressive, and prone to violence. Allstate clearly recognized that they had a very troubled and dangerous employee on their hands, and, claimed the lawsuit, their only desire was to be rid of him, regardless of the danger that this meant for his future coworkers.

Calden was socially isolated. He lived in a large apartment complex, alone, surrounded by a few electronic gadgets and his television set. His free time was spent playing video games on the personal computer he owned or endlessly watching television. A neighbor living near Calden's apartment said of his isolation: "I've never seen him with another human being, man or woman."[51] His reputation at work was the same, due primarily to his erratic behavior. Most of his interactions with coworkers were not warm; many were hostile. While at Fireman's Fund he would often engage in shouting matches with his coworkers or openly and vociferously challenge the authority of his supervisors. When he did not promptly receive a pay raise he thought he was owed, Calden threatened the company with a lawsuit. He shouted obscenities at a female coworker who inadvertently took his favorite parking spot and filed a formal harassment complaint against another colleague whose car sported a bumper sticker poking fun at his alma mater.[52] He was, by most opinions in the workplace, a distasteful and troubling person.

Repeating his behavior at Allstate, Calden often brought his handgun to work at Fireman's Fund in an effort to intimidate others. Key managers at the company realized that they must take some action to protect the work environment and terminated Paul Calden two years after they hired him. When he returned to Fireman's Fund to exact his revenge, Calden specifically targeted each individual who, in his mind, had participated in the decision to fire him.

Analysis

Paul Calden was a persistently angry, hostile man. As with many other workplace murderers, it is not difficult to perceive the emerging patterns of behavior that are so often the warning signs of a lethal employee (see Table 2.18). This is the advantage of hindsight—which is not available to workplace managers and supervisors who must make difficult decisions while embroiled in a potentially deadly situation. The actions of Allstate in buying Paul Calden out of its workplace may be considered dishonest or dishonorable, but they were certainly understandable. This get-him-out-at-any-cost approach to resolving the dangers presented by a potentially lethal employee is seen often among the incidents of workplace homicide. Imagine the fear, disbelief, and worry that accompanies the decision process in such a scenario as presented by an employee like Paul Calden.

Calden is another example of the classic workplace murderer—male, over thirty, white, socially isolated, and suffering the triggering event of losing his job. He also exhibited a history of violence—which is a strong predictor of future violence. His behavior at both Allstate and Fireman's Fund was clearly aggressive, intimidating, and hostile. It was reported, although not confirmed, that he once threatened a supervisor by throwing a chair at him. From what is known about Paul Calden's work history, his propensity toward violence escalated over the years from vocalization to action—a pattern that is frequently exhibited by the lethal employee.

It is also evident that Paul Calden suffered from chronic frustration and was a pathological blamer. Very minor frustrations, such as losing his favorite parking spot, were enough to push him to a violent reaction. All his social links existed in the workplace, an arena where he elected to intimidate and harass others, and consequently, where he received no acceptance. At home, Calden was completely alone, able to dwell persistently on the perceived wrongs he suffered. He lived a miserable and isolated life, attempting to make those around him as unhappy as he obviously was. In the end, his life had become meaningless, enabling him to carry out the ultimate act of revenge.

Table 2.18: Summary of Characteristics: Paul Calden

Male:	yes
Age range of 30-60 years:	yes
Evidence of social isolation:	yes
Evidence of triggering events:	yes
Vocalized violent intentions:	yes
Exhibited behavior uncomfortable to coworkers:	yes
History of violent behavior:	yes
Evidence of psychosis or psychological disorder:	no
Evidence of obsession or delusional disorder:	no
Alcohol or chemical dependence:	no
Severe or chronic depression:	no
Pathological blaming:	yes
Impaired neurological functioning:	no
Chronic or severe frustration:	possible
Preoccupation with weapons or paramilitary themes:	no
Evidence of severe personality disorder:	no

NOTHING FITS

Not all incidents of workplace murder carried out by an employee or ex-employee fit what has been learned about this crime from its decade-long public history. Although there are behavioral characteristics that can often be identified and categorized—and patterns of the crime that are familiar—some incidents defy all attempts at meaningful categorization and, in some cases, even a basic understanding of motive. Such anomalous cases are a troublesome and persistent characteristic of homicides committed by lethal employees. This is a clear indication that much has yet to be learned about the lethal employee, his behavior, and his motives.

The case of Christopher Green is a primary example of an incident of workplace homicide that defies all attempts at profiling the behavior of the perpetrator or even understanding the fundamental motive for his crime (see Table 2.19). There has been speculation that Green's motive was robbery and that the murders he committed resulted from his inability to control the situation; however, when the facts of the case are closely examined, this makes little sense. The perpetrator never attributed the murders specifically to the commission of another crime; that association was quite loose and appears to have been assumed in some press reports while excluded in others. When asked about why he murdered former coworkers as well as clients, Green was vague, remorseful, and imprecise about his reasons. He pled guilty to the crimes and was immediately sentenced, eliminating the possibility of a public trial, which could have provided more knowledge of the crime and the perpetrator. Christopher Green exhibited virtually no warning signs of potential violence, indicated no history that would lead one to suspect violence, and could only provide a vague motive for his crime—a motive that does not explain the nature and vehemence of his actions.

In a strict sense, the murders committed by Green do not comport with the definition of a lethal employee if one accepts a motive of robbery. However, if one rejects the implication that he committed murder in the pursuit of another crime, then his actions fit the definition of a lethal employee but lack an apparent motive or triggering event. This case is an enigma.

The Crime

Montclair is a comfortable community with strong, middle-class values. It is much appreciated by its residents for a progressive school system, safe neighborhoods, and a diverse demography. With a population of some 38,000, it is, in many ways, like a small city, replete with good jobs for its citizens and a bustling night life. However, in the few weeks preceding the Montclair Post Office murders, the community had experienced an unusual spate of crime. Two local teenagers had been arrested in the shooting of an elderly woman, and racial tensions had flared up at schools and between police and citizens on the south side of town. This was unusual for Montclair, but not nearly as shocking as the heinous crimes of Christopher Green would prove to be.

Christopher Green and his family were well known in Montclair. Green had lived in town nearly all his life, attended the local high school, and lived with a local woman in a fashionable, high-rise apartment building near the town center. Like his father before him, Green was hard-working, polite, and a man of his word. After graduating from high school, Green got a job with a local electrical contractor. He proved to be highly dependable and trustworthy, so much so that the business owner thought of Christopher as his own son, taking him along on family outings and spending time with him on frequent fishing trips. The local delicatessen where Green ate most days was happy to extend him credit as he needed it, knowing he would always repay his debts. By all accounts, Christopher Green was respected and trusted by all who knew him.

Green had always wanted to be a police officer or, failing that, a fireman. He studied diligently to take the examination for patrolman, and passed it. At the time he committed the murders at the local post office, Green was on the waiting list for openings at the Montclair Police Department. In March 1993, Green purchased a stainless-steel, .9-millimeter, Taurus handgun. He registered the gun as required by law and became proficient in its use. This was the weapon he would use two years later to slay four people.

From July 1992 until April 1993, Christopher Green worked at the Montclair Post Office as a janitor, being responsible for organizing and cleaning the premises each day. After that, he was able to secure a better paying job at the Montclair Department of Public Works (DPW) as a laborer. While working at the post office, Green, who made friends easily, became close to two career post office employees who also worked at the station. As was his history and reputation, Christopher Green was considered trustworthy and dependable by those who worked with him at the post office.

Table 2.19: Synopsis of Case Study No. 10

Perpetrator:	Christopher Green
Age:	29
Family:	Single (living with girlfriend)
Date of Incident:	March 21, 1995
Location of Incident:	Post Office (Montclair, NJ)
Employment Status:	Employed by Montclair Public Works. Previously employed by Montclair Post Office (1992-1993).
Work History:	Good to excellent performance history.
Criminal History:	None
Fatalities and Injuries:	4 killed, 1 injured
	Perpetrator survived and pled guilty to four counts of murder on June 8, 1995. Sentenced to multiple life terms, without parole, on September 22, 1995.

On March 21, 1995, Green left his DPW job in the late afternoon as usual. However, on this day he did not head for home. Instead, Green made his way to the nearby post office where he had previously worked. Arriving at the station just before closing time, around 4:00 in the afternoon, and entering through the front door, Green produced his .9-millimeter handgun and confronted the two employees and three customers who were on the premises. He was immediately recognized by the two employees, who were stunned to see their former coworker brandishing a weapon in their direction. This was completely uncharacteristic of the man they thought they knew so well.

When Green invaded the post office he had no disguise and was woefully unprepared for what appeared to be a robbery attempt. He demanded, and received, about $5,000 in cash from the employees; but he did not immediately leave the station. Green ordered his five hostages into the back room of the station and directed them to lie face-down on the floor. At least one of his former coworkers yelled his name and pleaded with him to leave. Instead, Christopher Green raised his .9-millimeter handgun and shot each, in turn, in the back of the head, execution style. Four of the individuals, including Green's two former coworkers, were killed instantly. One of the customers, although critically wounded, survived. Nearly an hour after the shootings, another postal employee, entering from the rear door of the station, discovered Christopher Green's victims and notified the authorities.

Green left the post office and returned to his apartment, stealing one of the victim's automobile to flee the scene. Once at his apartment, Green disposed of his bloody clothes in a gym bag, paid three month's back rent on his apartment, and stashed the remainder of the stolen money under the refrigerator.

Christopher Green was arrested the next day, just before noon, at his apartment. The Montclair police had received information from one of Green's acquaintances that he had been involved in the post officer murders. After running a computer search, law enforcement officials determined that Green was the registered owner of a .9-millimeter handgun, which was the caliber of weapon used in the killings. That was enough for them to issue a warrant and move quickly to locate the suspect at his apartment.

Police comments to the press indicated that Green was calm and cooperative when arrested, quickly admitting to the crime and describing in detail how he had murdered his former coworkers and the unfortunate customers. He then showed the police where he had hidden the rest of the money taken during the robbery—approximately $2,000 remained after he had paid the past-due rent. He also produced a gym bag, which contained the bloody clothes he had worn during the crime, three postal money orders, and thirteen rounds of ammunition.[53] During the police interrogation, when asked why he had murdered four individuals and critically wounded a fifth, Green only alluded to money he needed to pay the back rent due on his apartment. He had no plans for the extra $2,000.

Two days later Christopher Green was charged with multiple counts of murder and ordered to be held without bail. On June 8, 1995, Green pleaded guilty to the murders in a Camden, New Jersey, courtroom. He made few statements to the court but readily admitted his guilt and emphasized his feelings of remorse. When asked by Judge Joseph Rodriguez why he had executed four individuals in such a horrifying manner, Green replied: "I felt I was over the line, just at the point of no return. I was scared and I was confused."

Christopher Green was sentenced to life imprisonment without the possibility of parole. He made no subsequent statements about his motivation for the murders of March 21, 1995.

The Perpetrator

Christopher Green grew up in Montclair just a short distance from the post office where he executed four individuals and critically wounded another. Green's family was respectable, religious, hard working, and middle class.

Green's father was a maintenance man at an elite private school and described by all who knew him as a conscientious gentleman who instilled strong values in his son. Green attended the local high school in Montclair and was remembered by neighbors, many of whom had known him since birth, as an easy going, polite young man who was never in trouble. A long time friend of the Green family said this about Christopher: "He's never been in trouble; never done drugs."[54] Among the many press stories surrounding the crimes of Christopher Green in early 1995, none contradicted this opinion of him.

Table 2.20: Summary of Characteristics: Christopher Green

Male:	yes
Age range of 30-60 years:	no
Evidence of social isolation:	no
Evidence of triggering events:	possible
Vocalized violent intentions:	no
Exhibited behavior uncomfortable to coworkers:	no
History of violent behavior:	no
Evidence of psychosis or psychological disorder:	no
Evidence of obsession or delusional disorder:	no
Alcohol or chemical dependence:	no
Severe or chronic depression:	no
Pathological blaming:	no
Impaired neurological functioning:	no
Chronic or severe frustration:	no
Preoccupation with weapons or paramilitary themes:	no
Evidence of severe personality disorder:	no

In the 1980s, Christopher Green worked as an electrician's helper in town and quickly gained a reputation as an excellent worker. He was respected by his coworkers and generally regarded as a soft-spoken, hard-working gentleman with deep religious convictions. Green's reputation at the Montclair Department of Public Works, where he held a $26,000-a-year job as laborer, was the same. A local businessman, who had known Christopher Green since he was a child, echoed the opinion of all who knew him: "I don't understand how a boy this good goes bad. He must have snapped."[55]

Christopher Green had no criminal record at the time he committed the murders, with only a single minor offense committed as a juvenile. He had an excellent work history and had never been terminated from a job. Green lived in a comfortable, $800-per-month studio apartment on the sixteenth floor of a twenty-four-story high-rise building. At the time of the murders, he was living with a woman he loved. He appeared, to all who knew him, to be quite satisfied with his life; he had plans for the future, having passed the examination for the police department, and had secured a good job while waiting to come to the top of the list. If Christopher Green was experiencing any difficulties in his life, the only obvious one was that he was three months behind on his rent (see Table 2.20). After the murders, several press reports singled this out as a triggering event that may have driven Christopher Green to violence. That assessment remains problematic, although it obviously cannot be discounted.

Analysis

Is this a case of a robbery gone bad or retribution exacted by a lethal ex-employee? Post office officials were quick to deny the possibility of retribution, citing the time that had elapsed since Green worked at the post office and his excellent reputation while he worked there. He apparently had no motive that implied revenge or retribution. Green had never been accused of poor performance and he left the post office under good terms to take a more lucrative job. Initially, the majority of press reports pointed to robbery as a motive for the murders—nothing else made sense. Later reports, however, were less certain and more circumscribed as additional information about Green's background became available. He was, in every sense, a most unlikely perpetrator of robbery or murder.

Christopher Green exhibited virtually no warning signs that would point to potential violence. He was a man completely devoid of a history of violence, stable in his domestic life and at work, employed, not socially isolated, and apparently not addicted to drugs or alcohol. Green was trusted by coworkers and neighbors, even to the extent that he was allowed credit by local merchants, who knew he would repay his (minor) debts promptly and fully. He had been raised with strong family values and a sense of religion; he was not displaced during his life, and had definite plans for his future. There was no evidence of a psychological disorder, and he gave no indication of depression. In short, there would be no reason to expect Christopher Green to commit the crime of robbery, much less murder.

Green's murders could not be considered a crime of passion. He coldly executed four individuals who presented no threat to him. If the argument is made that he was afraid of being recognized as a robber by those who knew him so well, several counter questions must be posed. Why did Green disregard the obvious opportunity to rob the post office at a time when employees were not present? Why did he not use a disguise? Why would he even consider robbing a location where he was certain to be recognized? Was Green so inept, or the crime so unplanned, that he merely took the opportunity that afternoon to rob the post office? If that is true, why did he bring his handgun to work and stand by his typical work schedule?

It seems likely that Christopher Green made at least some effort to plan his crime. He knew that the best time to rob the post office would be at the closing hour. He planned ahead by bringing his weapon to work and leaving the crime scene in a vehicle other than his own. Green knew the layout of the station and was likely aware of the fact there would be cash available in a robbery. However, if all this is true, why did he find it necessary to execute his victims?

Although it cannot be denied that Christopher Green may have been motivated to rob in order to pay his back rent, one must question why he did not choose any number of other alternatives. He was a man with a good job, solid community reputation, and strong family ties; the rent he owed presented a difficulty that he could have easily overcome by more traditional means. There was little reason for him to resort to robbery—which was an act completely out of character based upon his life history up to that unfortunate date. Robbery is not an activity easily undertaken by an individual who had the background of Christopher Green. It is a crime most often undertaken by individuals who have a history of disregarding the law—something Green never did. Why, at this time, in this familiar place, and for a relatively small amount of money, would Christopher Green feel compelled to risk his well-planned future in such an extreme way?

The execution-style murder of Green's former coworkers and customers of the post office is incomprehensible in many ways. Green's crime was horrific, unnecessary, and brutal. It offered all the elements of a man who had lost control—who was exacting extreme revenge in a way that was clearly dissociated from those he personally knew. This, too, was completely out of character for Christopher Green. He was a man who made friends easily, trusted readily, and was respected in return. These were life values for Christopher Green; ones he would never give up easily or on a whim. He knew two of his victims very well and shared, at least, a bond of trust that naturally arose from a coworker relationship. At least two of his victims were individuals with whom he had no negative history and for whom he may have held positive feelings. However, he was able to slay these individuals as dispassionately as many lethal employees had slain other coworkers and supervisors before him.

This case is a sad, enigmatic addition to the history of occupational homicide. Whether, in the end, one considers this an incident in which employees and clients were slain in the course of another crime—the most traditional definition of occupational homicide—or some bizarre form of retribution or revenge that occurred for reasons not yet understood, the crimes of Christopher Green cannot be easily dismissed. There is simply nothing in his background or behavior that would lead one to expect him to resort to the violence he exhibited on March 21, 1995. Green, like many others, exemplifies the unpredictability of potential violence and demonstrates clearly that any effort at profiling the potentially lethal employee may prove to be dead wrong.

PICKED ON

When Willie Woods decided to take revenge at his place of work, he was very selective about who was to die—he targeted only those supervisors who he felt were responsible for his work performance difficulties. Woods believed he was about to lose his job and that four supervisors, in particular, were the real cause of his problems. He sought out each victim in a planned fashion, sparing the lives of other coworkers who happened to be in his path while ruthlessly murdering his predetermined victims (see Table 2.21).

The Crime

Willie Woods was a city electrician who worked at the C. Erwin Piper Technical Center, General Services Department, for twelve years. He was employed as a radio repairman in the sprawling, four-story complex, which housed some 300 city employees involved in various technical trades and criminal laboratory services supporting the city of Los Angeles. Woods's career went along smoothly until 1994, when he began to receive written warnings and verbal counseling about deteriorating performance. By mid-1995, Willie Woods had received at least five formal warnings about his poor work performance, two substandard work evaluations, and a notification of a formal hearing to determine if further disciplinary action should be taken against him. Despite this ominous set of circumstances, there had never been serious discussion of terminating Woods's employment, and such action had not been recommended by any of his supervisors.

Woods was clearly in deep trouble with his employer, and he was not taking it well. He was uncertain whether his supervisors intended to fire him, but he clearly believed they were acting against him in an unfair manner. Each time he was counseled about his performance, Woods would react with growing hostility and aggression. On at least one occasion, during a verbal counseling session, he picked up a chair and hurled it across the room. Woods also threatened each of the supervisors involved in discussions about his performance, even writing to one of the individuals at his residence. By the summer of 1995, it seemed that everyone knew Willie Woods had a significant performance problem and a virulent temper that was steadily spinning out of control. By July, the time for Woods's formal disciplinary hearing was approaching, and with each day, his threats became more ominous.

On July 19, 1995, Woods reported to work as usual, making his way directly to his workstation in the communications section of the large office building. As soon as he arrived at his desk, Woods became embroiled in an argument with another worker about a performance evaluation he had just received and his impending disciplinary hearing. He angrily left the work area, moving to another location where he stored his tools. Woods returned a few moments later brandishing a Glock semiautomatic pistol and a clip containing nineteen rounds of ammunition. It was approximately 10:15 a.m. when he began to search for the four supervisors who he thought responsible for his current·plight. Along his way, Woods encountered a number of coworkers, whom he simply ignored. Many, however, saw that he was carrying a large weapon in his hand and began to look for help.

Table 2.21: Synopsis of Case Study No. 11

Perpetrator:	Willie Woods
Age:	42
Family:	Unmarried
Date of Incident:	July 19, 1995
Location of Incident:	C. Erwin Piper Technical Center (Los Angeles, CA)
Employment Status:	Employed at the C. Erwin Piper Technical Center for 12 years.
Work History:	Good to excellent performance, including promotions, for over ten years. Deteriorating performance during the last 18 months.
Criminal History:	None
Fatalities and Injuries:	4 killed, none injured
	Perpetrator survived and was charged with 4 counts of murder.

Woods soon located two of the supervisors in their cubicles on the first floor of the communications center, where he shot and fatally wounded both at their desks. He then descended a flight of stairs to a lower level of the building, bypassing several coworkers whom he met along the way, to search for the last two supervisors. He encountered his third victim in the hallway leading from an office area. Woods raised his weapon and shot the man in the head and chest, wounding him fatally. Woods's final victim was sitting in his office when the perpetrator fired his final, lethal shots, again to the head and chest. The four supervisors, all men with many years of city service, would die from their wounds, one at the scene and three shortly thereafter at a nearby hospital.

Two law enforcement officers, who happened to be in the building on other business, heard the shots and were directed to where Willie Woods was last seen by coworkers. Woods attempted to escape by leaving the rear of the building and heading toward an open area at the rear of the complex through which railroad tracks passed west to the famous Los Angeles Union Station. The two officers pursued him as he ran toward the tracks and ordered Woods to drop his pistol and surrender. Woods quietly complied and was taken into custody without further incident.

Willie Woods was later arraigned and charged with four counts of first-degree murder with special circumstances. In California, these charges carry the death penalty upon conviction. On August 4, 1995, Woods pled not guilty to all charges.

The Perpetrator

Willie Woods was an ex-marine who had a history of good to excellent performance for over ten years at Piper Tech before he began to experience difficulties at work. During the first decade of his employment, Woods had received a promotion and consistently satisfactory performance evaluations. Throughout this period, Woods was described by coworkers as soft-spoken and easygoing. By 1994, Woods had received regular salary increases and was earning $44,000 per year plus a strong benefit package. In that year, however, things began to go wrong for Willie Woods.

Less than two years before the murders, Woods had purchased a home in Upland, San Bernardino County—an area that offered very comfortable homes in an upper-middle-class community. The home he purchased was impressive, with four bedrooms, a swimming pool, and a purchase price of $172,000. It was shortly after the purchase of this home that Woods's performance at work began to deteriorate for the first time since his employment a decade earlier (see Table 2.22).

As Woods's quality and quantity of work slipped, he was subjected to several verbal warnings, two substandard performance evaluations, and at least one formal disciplinary session. With each discussion about his performance, Willie Woods became more angry and hostile. He argued openly with his supervisors and frequently threatened them. He would publicly tear up and discard counseling documents and even throw furniture during the meetings. Following each counseling session, Woods's performance would deteriorate further and he would become more aggressive and intimidating to those in his presence.

When Willie Woods learned that he was to be subjected to a formal disciplinary hearing, he may have assumed that he was to be terminated. In fact, there were no such plans by any of his supervisors. Nonetheless, Woods was not communicating with his supervisors, and they were understandably reluctant to engage him in unnecessary conversation. By the day of the murders it appeared that Willie Woods was absolutely convinced that four of his supervisors were intent upon his termination and believed there was no point in further discussion. He was ready for revenge, had earlier brought a weapon to the workplace, and knew where and when to attack his victims.

Analysis

After a decade of solid performance, Willie Woods became caught in a web of stress and frustration that led eventually to murder. For whatever reason—perhaps initially because of the purchase of an expensive home and its attendant costs—Woods's ability to function effectively in the workplace quickly slipped away. His reactions to criticism were extreme and unpredictable. Individuals who knew him in the workplace or in his neighborhood commented that he had been transformed from an easygoing individual to one with a short and violent temper.

The cycle of criticism for work performance, followed by a hostile reaction from Woods, was repeated several times during the six months before the shootings. With each encounter, Willie Woods became more aggressive and violent. His actions and conversation made it clear the he was a man who could quickly become violent. Woods had also focused his rage on four individuals who, he was convinced, were trying to railroad him out of his job. Whenever he vocalized threats, they were consistently directed against one or more of these four supervisors. It is reasonable to assume that Willie Woods had become obsessed with the ideation that these four longtime managers had conspired to deny him his livelihood.

Table 2.22: Summary of Characteristics: Willie Woods

Male:	yes
Age range of 30-60 years:	yes
Evidence of social isolation:	yes
Evidence of triggering events:	yes
Vocalized violent intentions:	yes
Exhibited behavior uncomfortable to coworkers:	yes
History of violent behavior:	yes
Evidence of psychosis or psychological disorder:	no
Evidence of obsession or delusional disorder:	no
Alcohol or chemical dependence:	no
Severe or chronic depression:	unknown
Pathological blaming:	yes
Impaired neurological functioning:	no
Chronic or severe frustration:	yes
Preoccupation with weapons or paramilitary themes:	no
Evidence of severe personality disorder:	no

The pattern of Woods's deteriorating work performance, as well as his extreme reactions, vocalized threats, and erratic behavior, indicate that, in the period preceding his crime, he became chronically frustrated at work and unable to cope with the stressors in his life. It is possible that a near-two-year period of frustration and stress began with the purchase of an expensive home, which may have led to unexpected financial burdens that Woods could not resolve. When his job performance began to deteriorate, Woods was unable to deal with criticism and reacted in an extreme manner, much like an individual unable to cope with the life challenges he was facing.

It appears that Woods's employer handled the personnel aspects of his deteriorating performance in a highly formal and starkly impersonal manner.

No doubt this was due to the fact that Woods was a civil service employee, and thus subject to the rigidity of a major city government. The inflexible and slow-moving method of most government agencies facing serious personnel issues is legend. In this case, it was obviously an enabling element to homicide. Since Woods clearly exhibited warning signs of potential violence over a significant period of time, one must wonder if the outcome would have been less violent had members of management made a conscious effort to intervene by use of counseling or an employee assistance program.

REVENGE A YEAR LATER

A year after Jerry Hessler was terminated from his job, he decided on revenge, taking his murderous rampage into the very homes of those against whom he held a grudge. Hessler's actions in attacking multiple coworkers in their own homes is a rare form of occupational homicide—a type of aggression very different than the more common crime known as spillover workplace violence, which is aggression enacted in the workplace because of domestic or personal disputes elsewhere. His murders were also especially heinous in their planning and intense element of revenge, which extended to even a very young child.

The Crime

Jerry Hessler worked in the credit card operations department of Bank One for about eighteen months before he lost his job. A nondescript worker with an equally nondescript career, Hessler had been harassing female employees at the bank for some time, and in October 1994, matters came to a head—Hessler was fired for cause.

For the next year, Jerry Hessler was without work, living alone, and very bitter. Several of his former coworkers at Bank One had been instrumental in Hessler's termination for harassment—a fact he could not forget. Hessler had lost his girlfriend, also a former coworker, to another bank employee and had little to do but ponder the injustices he perceived he had suffered at the hands of his former colleagues. On the evening of November 19, 1995, Hessler decided he would carry out the revenge he had so long desired. That night he armed himself with a handgun, donned a bullet-proof vest under his jacket and planned out a driving route that would take him to the homes of those he so deeply despised. It was a Sunday night and he would arrive late at each home— a time when he was sure his victims would be accessible.

Hessler drove to the residence of Brian Stevens and his wife, Tracy. Mr. and Mrs. Stevens lived in Columbus with their two children, ages seven years and four months. Both Brian and Tracy were Bank One employees and former coworkers of Jerry Hessler. A third Bank One employee, Ruth Canter, was visiting with Mr. and Mrs. Stevens that evening. Arriving at the Stevens residence, Hessler broke into the house without warning and confronted the family. He quickly shot and killed Mr. and Mrs. Stevens and their four-month-old daughter and wounded Ms. Canter (see Table 2.23). The family's seven-year-old son hid during the melee and was uninjured. Hessler had carefully selected his first victims, who put up little resistance, and he wasted no time pursuing the next phase of his murderous plan.

Table 2.23: Synopsis of Case Study No. 12

Perpetrator:	Jerry Hessler
Age:	38
Family:	Single
Date of Incident:	November 19-20, 1995
Location of Incident:	Multiple locations (four) in and near Columbus, Ohio.
Employment Status:	Unemployed for one year.
Work History:	Terminated for harassing coworkers.
Criminal History:	None
Fatalities and Injuries:	4 killed, 2 injured
	Perpetrator survived.

Jerry Hessler drove north for a half-mile, arriving at the home of Mark Campolito, another Bank One employee and former coworker. Repeating the assault at the Stevens residence, Hessler broke into Campolito's home and shot him in the arm. He did not wait to determine the extent of Campolito's injuries, but hurriedly left the scene. Despite a significant loss of blood, Campolito survived the attack.

For reasons not understood by the authorities, Hessler then drove to the suburb of Worthington outside Columbus and broke into the home of P. Thane Griffin. Griffin, an unarmed, sixty-four-year-old male, was not a Bank One employee or former coworker of Hessler's, but rather a well-known charity executive in the area. For reasons unknown to anyone but Hessler, he shot and killed Griffin in his home.

Hessler now headed northeast. Driving for about seventy miles in search of his final victims, Hessler headed for Ashland and the home of his former girlfriend (now married), Judy Stanton. When Hessler arrived at the Stanton home, he banged loudly at the door but was refused entry by Mrs. Stanton and her husband. Furious, Hessler fired three shots at the Stantons' front door and kicked it off its hinges. Stepping inside with his handgun poised to fire, Hessler was confronted by Mr. Stanton, who was armed with two handguns of his own. Stanton immediately opened fire on Hessler and hit him directly in the chest; however, Hessler was still wearing the bullet-proof vest he had donned earlier.

Stunned but uninjured, Hessler fled the scene, leaving the Stanton family unhurt.

Hessler tried to flee the area, but law enforcement officials were, by now, in pursuit of him. Jerry Hessler was arrested before he was able to leave Ashland. He was subsequently charged with three counts of aggravated murder and two counts of felonious assault.

The Perpetrator

Very little is known about Jerry Hessler's background. He had no criminal record and no history of violence at the time of his termination from the bank credit card center. He had worked for Bank One for less than two years and had run into problems soon after he was hired. A thirty-eight-year-old, bespectacled, and taciturn man, Hessler kept almost exclusively to himself after the separation from his girlfriend. The particular target of Hessler's incessant harassment was, however, Tracy Stevens—his first victim.

After Hessler was fired from his job in October 1994, he continued to harass and threaten Tracy Stevens. Although this harassment took place via anonymous communications, Stevens knew it was Hessler and was clearly frightened. She reported Hessler's activities to her employer, Bank One, and was offered protection while traveling to and from work. She declined the offer and told her employer that she planned to contact police on the following Monday. Tragically, Tracy Stevens was slain by Hessler the preceding Sunday night.

Analysis

The crimes of Jerry Hessler are particularly disturbing because they occurred in the homes of his victims—a highly unusual venue for the lethal employee. It is evident that Hessler carefully planned his crimes and fully intended to carry out his revenge in the most heinous manner. His actions in killing the Stevens family, including their four-month-old daughter, are especially disturbing. The fact that Hessler drove for several hours in search of his victims, stopping at four different locations, evidences his absolute determination, planning, and callous disregard for the lives of others. This high degree of planning and intense commitment to seek out his victims in multiple locations is also unusual for a lethal employee.

Jerry Hessler's motivations were complex and still are not well understood. His actions prior to the slaying of Tracy Stevens and her family indicate a deep and abiding revenge focused upon specific coworkers who he believed had been responsible for the loss of his job. He had harassed Stevens persistently until the night he murdered her. It seems reasonable to assume that Hessler was obsessed with thoughts of revenge against Mrs. Stevens—a revenge so deep and all-encompassing that anyone in her presence must also die.

The attempted murder of his former girlfriend, Judy Stanton, indicates behavior consistent with that of a spurned lover, or actions similar to those often associated with the perpetrators of spillover workplace violence. It is clear that all but one of Hessler's victims, or intended victims, was a bank employee and former coworker who was somehow involved in the harassment charges that had led to Hessler's termination a year earlier. The slaying of Griffin, however, remains unexplained, and Hessler made no statement about it. There was no apparent relationship between Griffin and the incidents in late 1994 that led to Hessler's termination.

Table 2.24: Summary of Characteristics: Jerry Hessler

Male:	yes
Age range of 30-60 years:	yes
Evidence of social isolation:	yes
Evidence of triggering events:	yes
Vocalized violent intentions:	yes
Exhibited behavior uncomfortable to coworkers:	yes
History of violent behavior:	no
Evidence of psychosis or psychological disorder:	no
Evidence of obsession or delusional disorder:	possible
Alcohol or chemical dependence:	no
Severe or chronic depression:	possible
Pathological blaming:	unknown
Impaired neurological functioning:	no
Chronic or severe frustration:	unknown
Preoccupation with weapons or paramilitary themes:	no
Evidence of severe personality disorder:	no

It is clear that the triggering event for Hessler's murderous rampage was the loss of his job in October 1994. Subsequent to this, Hessler was socially isolated, unemployed, angry, and possibly depressed (see Table 2.24). He continued to harass at least one of his former coworkers and had much time to ponder his circumstances. When Jerry Hessler finally decided on a course of action, he was well prepared and had a definite plan. He was aware of the location of each of his victims and decided to attack them at a time when he could reasonably expect them to be at home. In each instance his attack was vicious; he was only stopped by the quick and decisive actions of one of his last intended victims, who was armed and ready to defend his family.

The disturbing nature of the crimes of Jerry Hessler, which involved attacking his victims in their own homes, adds a new dimension to the potential violence of the lethal employee. It is an especially frightening aspect to the crime of occupational homicide.

TRIGGERING EVENTS

In nearly every case of homicide perpetrated by the lethal employee, it is possible to identify one or more triggering events which are closely linked to a final act of murder. Often, there are a number of incidents that combine to destroy the perpetrator's ability to cope with a long period of frustration or anger. It is not unusual for a final triggering event to be relatively minor in nature yet perceived by the perpetrator as the final blow in a series of circumstances that inevitably leads to violent retribution. In other cases, the triggering event is significant and pernicious.

The case of Clifton McCree presents a vivid example of how a series of setbacks—triggering events—drove an individual with no history of violence or criminality to slay five individuals in an indiscriminate act of mass murder. McCree killed his former supervisor, several coworkers he had known for years, and one worker he had never met, all in a final act of frustration and retribution for losing his job. His brutal and methodical crime can be clearly linked to a series of events that apparently destroyed his ability to cope with the stressors in his life and drove him to murder and suicide (see Table 2.25).

The Crime

In December 1994, Clifton McCree had been employed by the city of Fort Lauderdale for eighteen years. He was a member of the city Hurricane Crew, a park department work crew locally renowned for their cleanup efforts following hurricane Andrew in 1992 and tropical storm Gordon in 1995. This twenty-three-member crew was housed in a blue and white municipal trailer located a block from the famous Atlantic Ocean Beach in Fort Lauderdale, just a few hundred yards from a spectacular neighborhood of multimillion-dollar homes overlooking the ocean.

After nearly two decades of good performance, Clifton McCree failed a routine drug screening when the test proved positive for marijuana use. As a result of the drug test, McCree was notified that he would be suspended from his job for twenty days. When McCree learned of the proposed disciplinary action, he reacted with hostility and anger, threatening coworkers and his supervisor. His anger was so deep that he even took to making rude comments to tourists and other members of the public using the nearby beach facilities.[56] Based on his failure to pass the drug test and his threatening behavior, Clifton McCree was eventually fired from his job, on December 9, 1994.

Prior to his termination, McCree had been offered drug counseling through an employee assistance program. He angrily refused the offer, and the issue was pursued no further. When confronted at his termination hearing about the threats he had made against his supervisor and coworkers, McCree called them "jokes" and said they were meaningless.[57] Among the threats McCree characterized as "meaningless" was a statement that he would return and "kill everybody" with whom he had worked.[58]

Table 2.25: Synopsis of Case Study No. 13

Perpetrator:	Clifton McCree
Age:	41
Family:	Married, father of three children.
Date of Incident:	February 9, 1996
Location of Incident:	Work site trailer (Fort Lauderdale, FL)
Employment Status:	Terminated after 18 years of service. Partially employed for 14 months prior to the crime.
Work History:	Stable until terminated. Terminated for failing to pass a drug test and making threats to his supervisor and coworkers.
Criminal History:	None
Fatalities and Injuries:	6 killed, 1 injured
	Perpetrator committed suicide at the scene.

Exactly fourteen months after he lost his job, Clifton McCree returned to his former workplace. Arriving at the park department trailer just before 5:00 in the morning, McCree was armed with a .9-millimeter semiautomatic handgun and a .32-caliber revolver holstered under his jacket. As he approached the trailer, several members of the Hurricane Crew were sitting at a table inside the temporary offices, chatting and preparing for the day's work. McCree entered the facility, displayed the .9-millimeter handgun, and ordered the workers to huddle in a corner of the office. He shouted, "Everyone is going to die," and began to open fire on the terrified employees.[59]

McCree rapidly and methodically shot each worker in the head as they tried to scramble for some protection inside the small office. Stopping to briefly reload his weapon once, McCree made sure each worker was dead with multiple shots to the head and torso. During the melee, one worker was able to escape through the back door of the trailer and call for help. Another of McCree's victims survived the attack by pretending he was dead from the two gunshot wounds he had received.

At the end of his rampage, McCree turned the .9-millimeter handgun on himself and committed suicide at the scene. He had fired off fourteen rounds from the same weapon, never using the still-holstered .32-caliber revolver. Among the dead were McCree's former supervisor and several coworkers. One of the slain, however, was unknown to McCree. She had only joined the Hurricane Crew a few months prior to the shooting. Inside Clifton McCree's pocket, law enforcement officials later found a suicide note he had written the night before the murders.

When speaking to the media after the incident, one employee who knew McCree said of him, "He made threats to come back and do things." Another said, "He thought everybody was out to get him . . . Just paranoia, I guess."[60]

However, most who knew McCree from his neighborhood never suspected he could resort to murder.

The Perpetrator

Clifton McCree served as a marine from 1975 to 1977. His military record was unblemished, and he had been awarded a medal for marksmanship during his service. After leaving the military, McCree joined the Fort Lauderdale public works department and was eventually assigned to the Hurricane Crew.

McCree lived with his wife and three children in a working-class neighborhood in Fort Lauderdale. Friends and neighbors described him as a pleasant, quiet man who kept mostly to himself.[61] He had no criminal record and worked steadily at his city job for nearly two decades. According to family members, McCree occasionally used marijuana throughout his adult life.

After McCree lost his job in December 1994, he struggled to find work. According to McCree's wife he became despondent after losing his job—a state of mind that worsened considerably just prior to the murders. McCree was eventually able to find part-time work as a security guard, but his income was insufficient to cover the family expenses. He left this job just three weeks before the murders and apparently spent the final few weeks of his life isolated in his home, deeply depressed and angry.

Mrs. McCree worked as a cook for several years, but she also lost her job, due to health problems. Just before the shootings, the water heater at the McCree household failed and McCree was unable to have it repaired—the family had no money. Clifton McCree sent his wife and children to live with his mother-in-law so they would at least be able to have a hot shower. After the killings, a relative of Clifton McCree described his state of mind during this final period: "People lose their heads when they lose their job, their livelihood. He didn't know what to do. [He was] losing everything."[62]

Clifton McCree's benign reputation in the neighborhood was quite different from that among his coworkers—at least during the period immediately preceding his termination in 1994. The sister of one of his victims claimed her brother often said that McCree was a dangerous man who reacted in unpredictable ways. Her brother had allegedly asked city officials on several occasions, particularly in recent months, to monitor McCree's actions in case he planned to return to his former workplace seeking revenge. McCree's victim once told family members, "If you ever get a call [from the police], this is the man who killed me."[63] Ironically, the worker who made this statement was the one who managed to survive McCree's vicious attack by pretending that he was dead.

Analysis

Clifton McCree was a middle-aged, African-American male who had recently lost his job of nearly two decades. He was not socially isolated prior to the loss of his job, although he was described by neighbors as a quiet individual who kept to himself. He was known to use marijuana but had no history of violence or other addictions. It is uncertain what role his use of marijuana played in the crime, but there is some evidence to suggest it may have been an integral factor. Although marijuana can induce anxiety and aggressive behavior in some individuals, as it may have with McCree, this is not a common reaction to the substance, which more often causes lethargy and feelings of euphoria.

It is clear from the case history that McCree became deeply depressed after he lost his job. He was also obviously angry and frustrated, both prior to his termination and afterwards. Given the fact that Clifton McCree held his job for eighteen years, it can be assumed that this was a critical component to his sense of wellness and crucial to his need to help support his family. There was no indication of difficulties at work prior to the incidents leading to his termination in late 1994. When he failed a drug test, McCree reacted with intense anger and growing frustration. He was apparently offered counseling for the drug use but refused the opportunity. Responding to his suspension for drug use with threats and intimidating behavior, McCree sealed his fate with the city, resulting in his termination exactly fourteen months before his crime of mass murder.

McCree's termination from his job signaled the beginning of a series of triggering events that led to homicide. According to coworkers, McCree was overtly hostile at the time of his termination; he was also despondent and depressed at home (see Table 2.26). He then suffered a long period of unemployment and was only able to find part-time work as a security guard. This was a job that paid very little—significantly less than he earned while working for the city. McCree was unable to contribute to the support of his family in a meaningful way and unable to find a job comparable to the one he had lost. Mrs. McCree also lost her job during this period and was suffering from significant health problems. The McCree family was financially devastated—so much so that they were unable to repair their water heater when it failed. McCree was forced to move his family out of their home to live with a relative in order to provide the minimum necessities. Throughout this period McCree became more depressed and was finally unable to keep his job as a security guard.

It is clear that Clifton McCree was a man who, in his mind, had little left to lose by early 1996. His lifestyle and that of his family had been completely disrupted by the loss of his job. He had no outlook for the future and was deeply depressed and chronically frustrated; he may have still been using marijuana on the day of the murders, although this is not certain. When he returned to his former workplace to exact revenge, McCree had already planned his own suicide and placed a final written message in his pocket to be found after his death. Clifton McCree had decided there was nothing left to live for and he was intent on destroying the organization he blamed for the disintegration of his life.

Table 2.26: Summary of Characteristics: Clifton McCree

Male:	yes
Age range of 30-60 years:	yes
Evidence of social isolation:	yes
Evidence of triggering events:	yes
Vocalized violent intentions:	yes
Exhibited behavior uncomfortable to coworkers:	yes
History of violent behavior:	no
Evidence of psychosis or psychological disorder:	no
Evidence of obsession or delusional disorder:	no
Alcohol or chemical dependence:	possible
Severe or chronic depression:	yes
Pathological blaming:	yes
Impaired neurological functioning:	no
Chronic or severe frustration:	yes
Preoccupation with weapons or paramilitary themes:	no
Evidence of severe personality disorder:	no

The history of frustrations, disappointments, and triggering events that impacted Clifton McCree between December 1994 and February 1996 are certainly no excuse for his heinous crime. The history does, however, clearly demonstrate how a series of events of sufficient moment can escalate the downward spiral of frustration and anger that is so often seen as a precursor to violence or murder. Clifton McCree had obviously planned his final actions. He possessed the weapons he needed for revenge, was proficient in their use, and was isolated from his family and friends just before the murders. Without any work or significant social contact during the weeks preceding his crime, McCree was completely absorbed in his depression and anger. Unable to cope with the significant setbacks he had recently experienced and seeing no way out of his dilemma, Clifton McCree made the decision to exact a final revenge on those he had threatened more than a year before.

A YEAR OF THE LETHAL EMPLOYEE

The case histories presented here provide only a small cross-section of the actions and impact of the lethal employee. There are many other murders committed each year by an employee or ex-employee driven to revenge. Here are a few additional examples of this crime that indicate its pervasive and destructive nature. Each of these incidents took place after January 1, 1995. In a few of the crimes, the victims survived the attack thanks to the immediate and effective action taken by local law enforcement and medical service personnel; however, in the majority of these cases the victims were not so fortunate:

Additional Examples

February 6, 1996, Honolulu, HI. John Miranda, an employee at an industrial company, returned to his former workplace after being fired from his job the previous week. He held five coworkers hostage, including his former supervisor, for up to six hours. During the incident, Miranda shot and seriously wounded his former supervisor and slightly wounded another coworker. The perpetrator was eventually killed by police after holding a shotgun to the head of one coworker for several hours while negotiating with officers by means of a cellular telephone. Prior to being shot by police, Miranda threatened to kill his hostage by starting a sixty-second countdown to pulling the trigger of the shotgun. This prompted the hostage to grab the barrel of the gun and gave police the opportunity to shoot Miranda, who died of his wounds. The perpetrator was angry about losing his job and had threatened revenge against the company and its workers.

December 15, 1995, Evendale, OH. Gerald Clemons, fifty-three, of Cleveland, returned to the Trans-Continental Systems offices from which he had been recently fired. Brandishing two pistols, Clemons shot and killed three employees and wounded a fourth. A witness stated that Clemons was "going after someone who had screwed him over"—his supervisor.[64] After the murders, Clemons surrendered quietly to authorities.

October 7, 1995, San Jose, CA. A junior accountant who had been on the job for only six weeks shot and killed his female supervisor and then committed suicide with the gun, one day after receiving his first performance counseling session. The killer was a twenty-eight-year-old Asian-American male; the victim a thirty-two-year-old Caucasian female. The perpetrator was apparently angered about the performance review, despite the fact it was not considered a negative one. When he reported to work at 7:30 a.m. the day after the counseling session, he went directly to his supervisor's office and fired several shots, killing her instantly. Without speaking, he immediately turned the gun to his own head and pulled the trigger. Officials at the company indicated that the accountant was not in trouble and in no danger of being terminated from his job. He was considered friendly but quiet, although no one at the organization knew him well because he had only been recently hired.

August 29, 1995, Palatine, IL. A postal worker reported to the workplace with a handgun and shot two coworkers who he claimed were his friends but with whom he had a disagreement. The shooter was a fifty-three-year-old Caucasian male who had worked at that same location for about twenty years and had "an exemplary service record."[65] The perpetrator's attorney stated that he had been under a doctor's care for depression and physical problems at the time of the shootings. The postal inspector, who knew the perpetrator, stated he was "a loner, a quiet individual," while one of his coworkers described him as a "beautiful guy."[66]

July 10, 1995, City of Industry, CA. A quiet, unassuming postal worker who had been on the job for twenty-two years shot and killed his supervisor.

The perpetrator was fifty-eight years old; he was easily disarmed by coworkers after the shooting. The victim was fifty years old and had apparently been in a dispute with the perpetrator. Just prior to the murder, at 2:30 a.m., the two men had argued, ending with the perpetrator punching his supervisor in the back of the head. When the supervisor left the area to report the incident to management, the perpetrator left the office area and returned with a .38-caliber revolver hidden in a paper bag. As the supervisor returned to the scene, the perpetrator pulled the handgun from the bag and shot his victim twice, killing him instantly. Interviewed after the incident, the perpetrator's coworkers and neighbors were shocked that a man with such a mild demeanor could have committed murder. The perpetrator lived alone in a middle-class neighborhood and was well known for his gentle disposition and kindness to stray animals.

May 18, 1995, Asheville, NC. An employee described as a "classic loner," who had just been fired from his job at a machine tool company, returned the next day with a rifle and a pistol. The perpetrator, who was forty-seven years old, killed three workers and wounded another four before surrendering to police. Several coworkers had expressed their concerns about the perpetrator's erratic and aggressive behavior before the murders.

April 27, 1995, Richmond, CA. After a housing authority employee learned he was to be fired from his job, he angrily left the offices, ostensibly heading to his automobile to leave the premises. Instead of driving away, however, the employee retrieved a semiautomatic handgun from his car and smuggled it back into the housing authority. He ran down the office hallway shooting at employees, apparently searching for the supervisor who had fired him. The perpetrator quickly located his former supervisor, shooting and killing her instantly. During the rampage he also shot and fatally wounded a coworker who was nearby. The perpetrator was a thirty-eight-year-old male receptionist who had worked for the housing authority for eight months. He had received a poor work performance evaluation, was currently on probation, and knew he was going to be fired from his job. Prior to the murders, he had vocalized threats against the agency and his supervisor, including a reference to the July 1993 shooting massacre of eight people at a San Francisco law firm. The perpetrator was arrested by law enforcement officials at the scene and later charged with two counts of homicide. The victims were two females, aged forty-seven and twenty-four years. It was later learned that housing authority officials were concerned about the possibility of a violent reaction from the receptionist and had requested extra police patrols to be stationed across the street from their offices. Unfortunately, there was no security present on the premises and the perpetrator was able to reenter the offices with his weapon.

April 4, 1995, Corpus Christi, TX. A former employee, twenty-eight years old, walked into a refinery inspection company and killed five employees with a handgun before turning it on himself. He was carrying a .9-millimeter semiautomatic pistol and a .32-caliber revolver. The perpetrator, James Simpson, murdered all the top executives of the organization. He had previously threatened coworkers and supervisors with revenge for losing his job.

March 12, 1995, Arlington, VA. A civilian Navy employee shot his supervisor and a coworker in their workplace before committing suicide with the same handgun. The two men had apparently argued about workplace issues.

January 17, 1995, Sparks, NV. An employee who had been fired for sleeping on the job returned to his former workplace brandishing a pistol and showering multiple shots into the ceiling of the building. As panicked employees ran for safety outside the building, the perpetrator sought out and cornered his former supervisor, shooting him in the leg with a .9-millimeter semiautomatic handgun. The perpetrator then barricaded himself in the office for several hours until local police were able to subdue and arrest him. Because of the prompt response of coworkers and local law enforcement personnel, the injured supervisor was quickly removed from the scene and survived his wounds.

ABOUT THE CASE STUDIES

The case studies presented here are only a small sample of the many incidents of murder perpetrated by the lethal employee over the past decade. They are, however, representative of the motivations, triggering events, and methods of operation of the murderous worker. Such incidents clearly illustrate that the lethal employee is a continuing threat to the workplace; he has become more active and more deadly with each passing year. They also illustrate the points of similarity and elements of divergence inherent in this category of crime. Hopefully, these studies make clear that there is nothing simple about the motivations or actions of the lethal employee. His final violent outburst is often the culmination of many events and experiences that, together, push him to murder.

The general profile of the lethal employee is known and is reasonably consistent; his behavioral warning signs are generally recognizable and reliable. However, the difficulty in predicting an outburst of violence by any particular employee remains highly problematic. Many workers will display the potential warning signs of violence; many will fit the profile of the potentially violent or lethal employee. The history of the lethal employee indicates that very few workers will resort to murder, although many will engage in some form of violence. The obvious difficulty is in identifying which workers will act out their aggressions and, of critical importance, who will likely become the next lethal worker. At this point in our understanding of the motivations and activities of the lethal employee, such a fine degree of prediction is not possible.

For now, the best course available to any organization that is serious about violence prevention is to understand how an individual is driven to violence, how to recognize the warning signs that are so frequently linked to escalating violence, and how to implement an intervention program that can effectively stabilize a developing situation and avert a violent outcome. In this sense it is critical to understand the lethal employee to the greatest extent possible—an understanding that can be enhanced through a study of the history of the crime itself. This understanding is best achieved by an analysis of the incidents of employee-perpetrated murder that provide sufficient, objective detail about the perpetrator and the workplace. Frequently, however, details of the crimes of a lethal employee are scarce and inaccurate, while information about the perpetrator's background is often absent. Much of the data about such crimes is derived from media reports, which are typically heavy on sensationalism and light on facts. It is common for such reports to provide conflicting information, speculation, and lack of confirmed facts. It is also common for the victim organization to do what it can to sequester information about the crime from the public, thus prohibiting a detailed understanding of the dynamics of the workplace. Finally, many perpetrators do not survive their crimes, thus allowing no opportunity to understand either the individual or his motives.

In the end, one is constrained to examine the activities of the lethal employee after the fact, with little accurate information, while being compelled to make some attempt to predict his future behavior. This is a daunting, perhaps even impossible, task. Despite a growing understanding of why an employee murders his coworkers or supervisors, we have yet to determine even a relatively reliable way to predict when the next crime will occur or who will perpetrate it. Since the lethal employee is a member of the workforce, it is impossible to rely on prosaic security measures to guaranty safety—the potential murderer himself will, in many cases, benefit from this same security. Entirely new methods of prevention must be employed if the workplace is to be made safe from the killer within. These new tactics must rely, in part, upon the ability to recognize the developing potential for violence and intervene to stop the inevitable. However, with whom does one intervene, and when?

The ability to recognize who in the workforce would benefit from positive intervention and when such intervention should take place has improved because of our increasing understanding of the lethal employee through an analysis of his crimes. This ability is, however, far from perfect and remains unreliable. Tools provided by the behavioral sciences help to identify the potential for violence as well as key behavioral warning signs; the science of management permits us to recognize weaknesses in organizations and personnel management practices that enable potential violence; the science of sociology allows us to understand broad imperatives for violence that impact every American worker. We have made a start, but it is *only* a start. The challenge now is to push further in our growing understanding of the lethal employee while ensuring that as many organizations as possible share in this knowledge and initiate their own prevention programs based upon what they have learned.

Case studies such as those presented here are an invaluable aid to understanding and training. They find particular worth in an organization that has made a commitment to violence prevention and needs to educate its staff about the issues of workplace violence and murder. Without question, case histories such as these do not make pleasant reading. The lethal employee is a vicious criminal who strikes out against those familiar to him and against those who may have even trusted him. The process of understanding his motives and actions can be difficult and painful. Still, murder committed by the lethal employee is not an abstract subject: it is a very real crime that threatens virtually any workplace in this country. An understanding of the crime and its perpetrator, which is best achieved by understanding his historical activities, is an essential first step in any violence prevention program.

NOTES

1. "Crazy Pat's Revenge," *Time*, 128, no. 9 (1 September. 1986): 19.

2. "10 Minutes of Madness," *Newsweek*, 1 September 1986, 42.

3. "David Burke's Deadly Revenge," *Time*, 21 December 1987, 30.

4. "Mass Murder in the Clouds." *U.S. News and World Report*, 21 December 1987, 14.

5. "Settling a Score." *Newsweek*, 21 December 1987, 43.

6. "Mass Murder in the Clouds," 14.

7. Linden Gross, "Twisted Love: A Deadly Obsession," *Cosmopolitan*, 213, no. 1 (July 1992): 190.

8. Ibid., 190.

9. Ibid., 190.

10. Tim Trebilcock, "I Love You to Death," *Redbook*, 178, no. 5 (March 1992): 100.

11. Ibid., 100.

12. Ibid., 100.

13. T. Stanley Duncan, "Death in the Office—Workplace Homicides," *Law Enforcement Bulletin*, 64, no. 4 (April 1995): 21.

14. "Another Fatal Attraction," *Time*, 29 February 1988, 49.

15. "Accused Slayer of 7 Tells of Obsession," *Los Angeles Times*, 21 August 1991, 20.

16. Ibid., 20.

17. "Jury Urges Death Penalty for Man Who Killed 7," *Los Angeles Times*, 2 November 1991, A27.

18. Ibid., A27.

19. Ibid., A27.

20. "Killer of Seven Gets Death in California," *Washington Post*, 18 January 1992, A9.

21. Trebilcock, "I Love You to Death," 100.

22. Ibid., 100.

23. American Psychiatric Association, *Diagnostic and Statistical Manual of Mental Disorders (DSM IV)*, 4th ed. (Washington, D.C.: American Psychiatric Association, 1994), 296-301.

24. Ibid., 297.

25. Trebilcock, 100.

26. *DSM IV*, 665-668.

27. J. A. Fox and J. Levin, *Overkill: Mass Murder and Serial Killing Exposed,* (New York: Plenum Press, 1994), 169.

28. Ibid., 171.

29. Ibid., 171.

30. Ibid., 171.

31. Ibid., 169-172.

32. Ibid., 186.

33. U.S. House of Representatives Committee on Post Office and Civil Service, *A Post Office Tragedy: The Shooting at Royal Oak,* (Washington, D.C.: U.S. Government Printing Office, 1992, 55.

34. S. Anthony Baron, *Violence in the Workplace,* (Ventura, Calif.: Pathfinder, 1993), 48.

35. U.S. House of Representatives, *A Post Office Tragedy,* 23.

36. Fox and Levin, *Overkill,* 188.

37. Ibid., 186.

38. Baron, *Violence in the Workplace,* 43.

39. Ibid., 43.

40. Ibid., 44.

41. John S. Cowan, "Lessons from the Fabrikant File: A Report to the Board of Governors of Concordia University," (Montreal, Canada: Concordia University, 1 May 1994): 13.

42. Ibid., 13.

43. Ibid., 19.

44. Ibid., 27.

45. Ibid., 27.

46. Fox and Levin, *Overkill,* 177.

47. Cowan, "Lessons", 29.

48. Fox and Levin, *Overkill,* 178-179.

49. Cowan, "Lessons", 9.

50. Fox and Levin, *Overkill,* 167.

51. Ibid., 179.

52. Ibid., 181.

53. Clifford J. Levy, "Former Montclair Post Worker Charged with Killings in Robbery," *New York Times,* 23 March 1995, A1.

54. Robert Hanley, "Co-Workers Are Stunned: 'No, It Couldn't Be True,'" *New York Times,* 23 March 1995, B7.

55. Ibid., B7.

56. "Six Dead in Ft. Lauderdale Shooting," *USA Today On-line,* Internet, 10 February 1996.

57. "Fired Employee Kills Five Co-Workers, Self," *Reuter's New Media,* Internet, 10 February 1996.

58. Florida Gunman Had Threatened to Return to Kill Co-Workers," *CNN Interactive,* Internet, 10 February 1996.

59. "Fired Employee Kills Five Co-Workers."

60. "Six Dead in Ft. Lauderdale Shooting."

61. "Family Said Gunman was Despondent." *Reuter's New Media,* Internet, 10 February 1996.

62. Ibid.

63. Ibid.

64. *Reuter's New Media,* "Daily News Summary," Internet, 16 December 1995.

65. *Reuter's New Media,* "Daily News Summary," Internet, 15 August 1995.

66. "Postal Worker Held in Shootings on Job." *San Francisco Chronicle,* 30 August 1995, A7.

3

Driven to Violence and Murder

A society that presumes a norm of violence and celebrates aggression, whether in the subway, on the football field, or in the conduct of its business, cannot help making celebrities of the people who would destroy it.

—Lewis H. Lapham
"Citizen Goetz" (Harper's, March 1985)

The history of occupational homicide in America demonstrates that the lethal employee is often a person who is driven to an extreme outburst of violence that is frequently unexpected and sometimes indiscriminate. His motives may be straightforward, but they can also be complex and covert. Incidents of workplace homicide vary in their extent of planning and execution, resulting in unpredictable devastation to the workplace. Occupational homicide by a coworker is not always a calculated crime; it is rarely carried out with surgical precision even if the perpetrator has a specific goal in mind. In some cases, however, it is precisely that—a well-planned execution or series of executions. Workplace murder perpetrated by the lethal employee is not a crime for profit carried out by a career criminal. In this sense the act will always be at least somewhat unpredictable. It may, at times, be a crime of opportunity and therefore subject to some standardized security and prevention measures. Without question, this form of occupational homicide is a crime of revenge and will therefore be infused with great passion and, frequently, an element of disregard for the consequences.

The lethal employee, once committed to murder, may not consider the ramifications of his actions beyond the general imperative of retribution, or he may target specific individuals to die but be quite careful not to injure others. Even though he may only target supervisors or members of management, once the rampage has begun, he may often still murder coworkers against whom he holds no grudge. If he kills indiscriminately, the mayhem he brings to the workplace can make the lethal employee a particularly onerous threat to *any* member of the workforce, and to the organization itself.

When an employee lashes out against his supervisors or coworkers in an indiscriminate manner, disregarding who is injured or killed in the process, he is attacking the entire organization. His symbolic effort is to murder the employer—to completely destroy the company. He has successfully depersonalized those around him who are potential victims, dissociated himself from the meaning of his actions, and focused his sole purpose—perhaps his own life—upon the symbolic destruction of the organization that is, or was, his employer. He may kill randomly only after attacking the primary targets of his revenge, turning his secondary rage against the organization; or his only intention may be to inflict the maximum penalty against the company through indiscriminate revenge.

The motivations of a workplace murderer are rarely as clear as the media tends to portray them. His actions may be planned, vaguely considered, or random; his targets may be specific, symbolic, or both. Even if the crime has been planned, the perpetrator will often injure or kill coworkers unfortunate enough to be in his path, despite an initial intent to avoid indiscriminate violence. When the crime is not well planned or the circumstances are not as he anticipated, which is often the case, the lethal employee will injure or kill individuals who were never the focus of his rage prior to its enactment.

There are no statistical databases in existence from which one can derive the apparent extent of the random killings that are often associated with workplace homicide carried out by the lethal employee. What information is available can only be drawn from what has been reported in the media and infrequent private or government studies. However, this aspect of the crime—its degree of randomness—can be generally categorized based on a study of the victims and how they died in incidents of occupational homicide. When this is done, three categories of workplace homicide perpetrated by the lethal employee arise.

Incident Type 1: Planned, nonsymbolic retribution. This could be defined as a *well-planned homicide targeting specific victims.* In this form of the crime, the lethal employee has clearly targeted certain individuals in the workplace, has typically planned his actions to minimize injury to himself and others, and will usually stop his actions voluntarily when his revenge has been appeased or the plan has been executed to his satisfaction. On occasion, this perpetrator will commit suicide and, if he does, it will probably have also been planned in advance (as in the case of Paul Calden); however, he is more likely to voluntarily surrender to others upon completion of his crime. Incidents of this type are frequent. If poorly planned, this form of specific retribution can degenerate into a type 2 incident discussed next. The nonsymbolic incident is easily identified because of its obvious planning, which is often indicated by the actions of the perpetrator days, or even months, before he acts. There will be a relationship between the perpetrator and his victim or victims that is obvious and strained. The theme of revenge or retribution will be equally obvious and will often be vocalized by the perpetrator prior to, and during, the commission of his crimes. Cases such as that of Paul Calden, who specifically targeted certain executives, or Willie Woods, who targeted only certain supervisors, are examples of this incident type. These crimes demonstrate planning, selectivity, and an obvious unwillingness to victimize coworkers or clients not specifically targeted by the murderer. In the case of Paul Calden, the strategy also involved planning his suicide at a predetermined site, including selecting his means of transportation.

Incident Type 2: Poorly planned retribution with symbolic qualities. This could be defined as *homicide targeting both specific victims and the organization.* This is a common form of workplace homicide, which can easily result in mass murder. In this incident type, the perpetrator has one or more targets against whom he will seek revenge; however, his intent is not focused, his planning is poor, and there will be overt symbolism demonstrated in the extreme violence of his actions. The crimes committed by Robert Sherrill at the Edmond Post Office, Richard Burke aboard a PSA flight in California, or Richard Farley at ESL Corporation are primary examples of this form of workplace homicide. The perpetrator of this incident type is frequently driven to a degree of violence that is extreme in its impact. He may exhibit multiple behavioral warning signs or suffer from a significant psychological disorder which has been in evidence for some time before he commits to violence. He will specifically target one or more victims in the workplace, but he will not stop with these individuals. He may continue to kill randomly after attacking his primary targets or may murder coworkers in his path in an effort to reach his primary targets. Although the perpetrator may survive his actions, there is a high probability that he will commit suicide at or near the scene of the crime. Upon examining his actions at the crime scene there will likely be significant evidence of symbolic destructive behavior directed at the organization in general.

Incident Type 3: Random, symbolic retribution. This could be defined as *unplanned homicide symbolically targeting the organization without regard to specific victims.* This incident type is relatively rare among cases of workplace homicide. It is most likely to occur when planning is absent or, occasionally, when the perpetrator carries on with his plan despite the absence of the individuals whom he considered as targets. The perpetrator of this form of the crime often suffers from a severe psychological disorder, will probably exhibit the warning signs of psychosis, and is unlikely to survive his actions. This category should explicitly exclude incidents of terrorism or homicide perpetrated for political or economic motivations—violence that should be considered in a far different criminal genre than that examined in this book.

A careful review of incidents of occupational homicide over the past decade leads to the conclusion that most incidents are of Type 1: Planned, nonsymbolic retribution, followed by Type 2: Poorly planned retribution with symbolic qualities, with Type 3: Random, symbolic retribution identified as a rare event. This is, of course, a speculative conclusion and not based on good statistical evidence. In most incidents, however, there is a general pattern that can be discerned, leading to the ability to categorize incidents of occupational homicide.

The lethal employee will typically target one or more individuals against whom his desire for revenge is great. Although he often *desires* the complete destruction of the organization, the perpetrator will typically focus upon certain individuals to the exclusion of others; his primary targets will most likely be supervisors or members of management, although they may be coworkers against whom he holds a long-standing grudge. When he enters the workplace intent upon retribution he will often seek out his primary target first. To this point, his crime will have been planned. However, many lethal employees will not stop with retribution against their primary victims.

For many workplace murderers, the overwhelming goal is to symbolically destroy the overriding target of their frustration and anger—the organization. When this is the lethal employee's state of mind, all coworkers are at risk, as well as clients and other individuals not directly associated with the target organization. In many of the case histories in this book, the perpetrator targeted both specific individuals and the organization itself. This form of workplace homicide, Type 2: Poorly planned retribution with symbolic qualities, is frequently associated with acts of multiple or mass murder and has become increasingly common in recent years. It is also common for the perpetrator of this type of incident to commit suicide or induce his own death at the scene of the crime. This willingness to die in an act of revenge lends an especially desperate and heinous quality to the crime. It also enormously complicates efforts at intervention or prevention.

For the purposes of planning intervention or prevention programs, it must be assumed that the lethal employee will not only strike against specific individuals but will also attempt to symbolically annihilate the organization itself. This is a painful and unwelcome assumption because it is difficult to accept. Nonetheless, the history of occupational homicide demonstrates that the lethal employee is as likely to randomly kill coworkers as he is to specifically target individuals against whom he holds a grudge. When assessing the potential for violence presented by an employee, one can sometimes discern the extent to which he is considering retribution. The individual may make specific and repetitive threats against certain coworkers or supervisors, or he may threaten the organization on a broader basis. Even though this kind of information may be helpful in providing protection in the workplace, it cannot be considered reliable. If and when the potentially lethal employee begins to act out his revenge, he may kill randomly despite his own predisposition to avoid doing so. Recognition of the potential danger of the situation, accompanied by an effective response, must occur very early in the cycle leading to violence if prevention is to be effective. The most efficacious prevention program will recognize the imperatives for violence that transcend individual circumstances and form the very basis for a potentially violent response by any individual in the workforce.

IMPERATIVES FOR VIOLENCE

How an employee is finally driven to an act of violence or homicide is a complex and much-debated issue. The general imperatives for violence in our society have been discussed and analyzed voluminously and effectively in the past few decades; much has been learned about why certain individuals resort to violence. However, given the unwholesome fact that Americans have created and accepted an aggressive society, the need to understand why its citizens are so frequently violent remains a fundamental issue. The American workplace, which is an essential and integral component in the lives of most citizens, has evolved into an arena for violence and murder in lock step with the general increase in societal violence. In order to reverse this threat to the business community, any effort at workplace violence prevention must consider the imperatives for aggression that may motivate the violent or potentially lethal employee.

It is clear that such imperatives are many and complex. It would be a monumental, and likely impossible, task to attempt to assemble *all* imperatives into a form that would receive a general consensus. Nonetheless, it is important to at least identify the key imperatives for violence that clearly affect the majority of the American workforce and that, on the part of some employees, combine to induce or enable acts of violence.

It is known from a decade-long history of workplace violence and occupational homicide that the overwhelming majority of violent or lethal employees are male; they are most often members of the baby-boomer generation—individuals who share a common compendium of hopes and expectations intermingled with strikingly similar disillusionments and frustrations. This generation is estimated to be approximately 76 million strong, and it constitutes the heart of the American workforce. Its members have experienced unprecedented postwar comforts and unexpected change within their personal lives and careers. This generation has been caught up in national and global transformation of unimagined proportions. As beneficiaries of an unparalleled availability of information about their society and the world in general, it is not surprising that baby boomers are especially impacted by societal imperatives in many forms, including those that imply or enable violence.

An understanding of the imperatives for violence that affect employees, when used in combination with the evolving profile of the violent or potentially lethal employee, adds considerably to the efficacy of intervention programs designed to break the chain of events and reactions that can result in violence or murder. These imperatives do not affect all workers in the same way; nor do employees react to them in predictable ways. They do, however, affect all workers in some manner. A supervisor, health-care provider, or employee representative who is aware of the inordinate impact on an employee of one or more of these imperatives may be presented with an opportunity for intervention that could divert future violence.

What follows is, by no means, a comprehensive list of the many imperatives for violence that affect the American workforce. They are, however, fundamental factors that can drive certain employees to violence if they are not mediated and overcome in positive ways. At a minimum, they represent elements that should always be considered when evaluating the potential for violence because, in one form or another, they have often been identified as enabling components when trying to understand why an employee has acted out his aggressions in the work environment.

Societal Imperatives

Unexpected legacies of the late twentieth century. The end of World War II engendered a new and remarkable chapter in U.S. history. This era, which was distinguished by the emergence of the baby-boomer generation, was one of unprecedented transformation and unrelenting instability. Despite the promise of the late 1940s, many in this generation became steeped in disillusionment, pervasively distrustful, and driven to survival rather than becoming the beneficiaries of opportunity as they had anticipated. Certainly, none born to this era could avoid the relentless waves of change and instability that swept through the postwar decades and continues today. The era began with uncommon hope and yet ended with unparalleled disillusionment. Its effect on many Americans was pernicious, as it served to completely eliminate the dream of a nation of peace and partnerships, which had seemed almost inevitable in the flush of national victory in 1945.

This country experienced an unequaled period of opportunity and wealth immediately following World War II. Throughout the late 1940s and into the 1950s, at the height of the baby boom, Americans settled into a growing economy that was able to provide meaningful, stable employment. Rapidly developing suburban neighborhoods offered a safe and rewarding domestic life. Technology was changing rapidly, promising ease, luxury, and opportunities for a prosperous future. The domestic vision of America was one of a strong nuclear family benefiting from a rigorous economy and moving inexorably toward a future of even greater stability and leisure. Children born into this period were not only numerous, they experienced early years filled with the idealistic vision of a nation free from war, economically sound, and blessed with a tomorrow rich in possibilities. The American dream of a meaningful career and a secure, comfortable home environment seemed guaranteed. Unfortunately, however, it was a short-lived legacy.

As memories of the war grew distant, new and profoundly disturbing threats to the national dream became apparent. America found itself locked in a virtual death struggle with other nations over opposing ideologies. National assets and energies were poured into an effort to protect American interests, and perhaps even the nation's survival, throughout the world; weapons of unprecedented technology and destructive potential were given a clear priority in a race to balance the structure of power among opposing nations. The pernicious effect of unhealthy domestic politics, such as McCarthyism, ripped open the fabric of trust and acceptance that had promised to finally take root at the end of the war. The need for backyard bomb shelters, a constant fear of global thermonuclear war, and the raging national arguments over the very meaning of America quickly dissolved the short-lived national dream in the harsh environment of a nation, and a world, experiencing unprecedented change on every front. The once-unquestioned ability of Americans to carve out their own destiny—to make their own way in a country that was strong and independent—had disappeared. America was now a member of the world community, and that community was, in many ways, still at war.

In the 1950s there was the Korean War; in the 1960s, the Vietnam War; and in the 1970s, an unrelenting number of localized conflicts designed to clearly establish an American role in world affairs. For the children of the 1950s, 1960s, and 1970s, there was little question that the world was a dangerous place and that America had changed significantly. A sense of distrust and disillusionment with the nation and its leaders became pervasive. The politics of the cold war left most Americans uncertain, suspicious, and deeply concerned about survival. Unpopular conflicts divided the country, dishonest leaders deceived their constituents, reports of domestic violence became rampant, and crime raged out of control across the nation. The fountainhead of stability in the late 1940s and 1950s—the family—disintegrated at an alarming rate across the nation. The politics of the nation became those of survival, not partnership. The concept of winning, regardless of cost, became a national obsession.

All the promise of the early post-World War II period had evaporated among the realities of America's changing role in the world community—there was an absence of clear, consistent, partnership-oriented national leadership. America had become a dangerous place; the world was even more so. The national obsession to win—to survive at any cost—stood at the shoulder of each baby boomer as he or she entered the workforce for the first time. Many children born into this era had witnessed the dissolution of their parents' dreams and saw firsthand that the nation they inherited was not a haven for opportunity and promise but rather an environment fraught with danger, deceit, and instability. They experienced a deep disillusionment with America even before they truly inherited the widespread economic and technological power they now possess.

For many millions of the baby-boomer generation, the accepted vision of America became one of uncertainty—a paradigm that could never comport with the dreams of their parents. The expectations of success and opportunity, which many believed to be their birthright, had been ripped away. In their place had been left the seeds of doubt, anxiety, anger, and frustration—the precursors of aggression for those unable to overcome such a dark legacy. Their birthright was a nation that they could not influence, a world too complex for their understanding, and a future laced with uncertainty.

A Culture of Aggression. Aggression is inherent in American society. Whether carried out in pursuit of profits, power, or entertainment, acts of aggression are rampant and often highly rewarded. This form of behavior has become, not only a national tradition, but also an expected legacy for each succeeding generation. Although the national fetish for aggression has been a longtime staple of American culture, this behavior has become even more pervasive and pernicious in recent decades, as is particularly evident in the entertainment industry.

By the beginning of the 1990s, the A. C. Nielson company reported that 98 percent of all American households had at least one television set operating for an average of four to eight hours each day.[1]   At the same time, the American Psychological Association estimated that the average seventh grade student had witnessed over 8,000 murders and 100,000 other acts of violence because of the programming flooding nearly every American household for so many hours each day. In other words, acts of violence and aggression were, by the start of this decade, the entertainment of choice for most citizens and their children; they were unavoidable. Because of the impact of television programming, violence and aggression have been transformed into an acceptable form of entertainment on a national scale. Worse, such programming enthrones violent behavior that is emulated by a vast viewing audience of children and adolescents.

In 1996, the results of a study funded by the National Cable Television Association examining the impact of violent television programming were released. This research indicated that 57 percent of all television programming contained some violence and that the perpetrators of this violence went unpunished for their actions 73 percent of the time.[2] The message inherent in this data is clear—violence on television is pervasive and represents a form of acceptable, or at least unpunished, behavior. A general desensitization to violence has been the legacy of our entertainment industry, which is acted out with alarming frequency on our streets, at home, and in the workplace.

Alarmingly, the escalating images of violence offered by the entertainment industry have been much enhanced by recent technological innovations. Weapons of every conceivable variety and detail, and often of mass destruction, are voluminously brought into the American home on television. Hero figures are frequently violent and aggressive. Commercial programming encourages parents to purchase mock weapons used by these hero figures, transforming the natural play of children into fantasy competitions of mayhem and death. There is little place in the entertainment industry for the hero who chooses partnership and nonviolence over winning at all cost. It is unlikely that our children will emulate the pacifist, philosopher, or peacemaker when he or she is rarely seen or hopelessly outnumbered by the vicious and the violent.

The entertainment industry, and particularly television programming, also provides the opportunity to learn. Unfortunately, much of what is learned can lead to violence. Criminal acts—particularly homicide—are enthroned with vivid detail and constantly expanding variations by the majority of commercial television stations as a daily routine. Any viewer can quickly learn about the weapons and tactics of violence in a way that completely disassociates the real-life implications of violence from the fantasy world of television or the cinema. The constant flow of aggressive imagery from the entertainment industry can, and does, provide all the elements needed by an individual who desires to choose a violent course—practical information, tactics, motivation, behavior, and a result that can be altered by fantasy, whether fair or foul. It rarely advocates the alternative behavior of understanding, cooperation, and partnership.

Financial stress. The ability to achieve and maintain a comfortable standard of living has, for many Americans, slipped away over the past few decades. Increasing costs of housing, medical services, transportation, clothing, education, and household necessities have eroded the standard of living for many millions of citizens. These Americans are working longer hours yet generating considerably less discretionary income than they ever expected. Millions have been forced to work in low-paying jobs with no future in order to maintain even a minimal standard of living. Millions more believe they have never attained the employment satisfaction they deserve, either in terms of career potential or compensation.

Since 1970, the number of Americans who have fallen below the national poverty level has steadily increased to its present number of over 36 million (see Figure 3.1). Many millions of other working Americans, while not officially at or below the poverty level, struggle for a modest, or even substandard, existence in jobs that pay the minimum hourly wage. In 1993, there were nearly twice as many hourly paid workers earning less than $10 per hour (40.6 million) as there were earning more than $10 per hour (22.7 million). More than 10 percent (4.2 million) of those earning less than $10 per hour were receiving a minimum wage of $4.25 per hour or less.[3]

Figure 3.1: Millions below the Poverty Level[4]

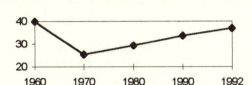

The 1990 census reported that even those Americans fortunate enough to be employed were not doing well. In that year, the median household income fell by 1.7 percent to $29,943 annually. On a per capita basis, real income for all citizens declined by 2.9 percent in 1990, to an average annual income of $14,387.[5]   While the general cost of living continued to increase across virtually every major expense category, average annual income dropped consistently for the three years preceding the 1990 census as American workers found themselves falling ever farther behind their dreams and expectations.

Throughout the 1980s and into the 1990s, the gap widened between those working Americans who had achieved some measure of prosperity and those who had seen their quality of life slip away. Long periods of pervasive unemployment in the early 1990s worsened matters for many millions of workers. Overall, for the vast majority of working citizens, the outlook for increasing real income has steadily diminished for the past few decades. For a vast number of citizens, the traditional American dream of home ownership and stable employment that produces discretionary income is simply unattainable.

For workers from the baby-boomer generation, which forms the mainstay of the American labor pool, the economic outlook is not bright. The basic expectation of a good reward for a good life's work has eluded many in this generation. Millions of middle-age employees will never experience the pleasures of a comfortable period of retirement—even those fortunate enough to maintain their employment until retirement age. For many, this is a shattered dream, which has been replaced by a desperate drive to simply maintain their present job at any cost. There is little reason to be optimistic about future employment opportunities.

These workers are now at or near the peak of their earning power and must maintain stable employment at a time in their life when expenses are running high. They are acutely aware that the financial stress caused by a job loss could prove catastrophic; they are also increasingly cognizant of the possibility of being displaced by younger, less costly employees. With little opportunity for a significant increase in their earning power, coupled with an awareness of the ever-present threat of economic catastrophe, these workers may take extraordinary measures to maintain their employment and income. They often feel threatened by any significant change in the work environment that may impact them economically. The increasing popularity of targeting workers in this age group to reduce costs or increase profits is seen, not only as the genesis of financial disaster, but as the act of an uncaring, disloyal employer.

The combination of a desperate need for continued employment and an uncertain and changing working environment is often identified as a significant triggering event in the actions of a violent or lethal employee. The years of frustration that can result from an inability to achieve an acceptable standard of living, compounded by the imminent threat of financial disaster brought on by the loss of a job, can result in a life situation that appears hopeless to the displaced employee. With little opportunity to replace lost income, a diminished possibility of quickly rejoining the workforce, and the inadequacy of national or state support systems for the unemployed, it should not be surprising that an increasing number of individuals who experience this situation lash out in violent acts of retribution.

Changes in the family. The typical middle-aged male worker in today's labor pool was probably raised in a two-parent household—the prototype of the American nuclear family. This was the norm for the majority of the baby-boomer generation; it implied a social standard that established lifelong expectations and assumptions, many of which have been invalidated in recent years. The perception of a male breadwinner, who was successful at work and effectively supported a nuclear family, has been swept away by shifting demographics and significant transformations in both the American economy and its citizens' lifestyle. Whether or not one considers these transformations an indication of progress, the old vision of the 1940s and 1950s remains with many male members of the workforce. They are unwilling or unable to accept the significant transformations that have impacted the American family and, in some cases, they are incapable of coping with the resultant changing or disintegrating relationships.

Many middle-age male employees are threatened by the increasing numbers of successful women in the workforce or the impact of national efforts at workplace diversity. They are uncomfortable with the changing structure of the family, the redefined roles of parents and children, and, perhaps, what they view as a loss of prestige or control over their domestic situation. Their role as the central support for a traditional family structure has been diminished at a time when their role in the workplace may also be uncertain and changing.

Figure 3.2: Children Living with Both Parents (Thousands)[6]

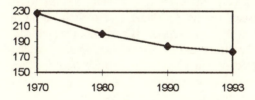

There is little question that the growing diversity of the American workplace is a positive and healthy trend. It is, however, painful for many, as is the evolving nature of the American family. To many middle-age males, who are the predominant perpetrators of workplace violence and homicide, it seems that their time-honored role as husband, father, and provider has been diminished or destroyed. They have been thrust into a new national culture which is changing rapidly and unexpectedly on both the domestic front and in the workplace. For some workers, those who find it impossible to relinquish their traditional roles, there is little respite from perceived threats at home and on the job (see Figure 3.2). For a few, these stressors evolve into triggering events for violence; acts of anger and frustration that may be predicated upon domestic difficulties but spill over into the workplace.

Compounding this situation is the increasing mobility of the American population. Many workers travel far from their close family members in pursuit of a career. Extended families living in close proximity are quickly becoming the exception where they were once the standard. The bond that once closely united family members is diminishing in importance or may have been sacrificed by economic necessity. The result of this mobility, whether by choice or circumstance, is to significantly reduce the close support network that is most often provided by family members. Alone or socially isolated, many workers who experience personal or work difficulties have a minimal or nonexistent support system; they lack family members to whom they can turn. One of the most prevalent characteristics of the lethal employee is his social isolation—his inability to turn to those close to him (usually family members) when support is desperately needed and violence could be prevented.

Social isolation. Social isolation is an enabling factor in many cases of workplace homicide committed by the lethal employee. Workers who have suffered the disintegration of domestic relationships, who live alone, or who lack close companions are more likely to react with violence than individuals who have a close and reliable support system available to them. With the weakening of the family structure and the increased mobility of the American population over the past few decades, social isolation has become a problem for many employees. Individuals often live far removed from their families or are displaced by a job transfer or period of unemployment. Organizations are also more mobile than in the past, adding to the social displacement and isolation that has become increasingly common in our society. When an individual must confront significant domestic and work-related stressors, it is often vital to have a close support network at hand—individuals with whom one can discuss troublesome issues, resolve problems, and reestablish an appropriate sense of self-worth. When this vital support is absent, an individual may easily become obsessed with the difficulties he is experiencing and unable to establish either a reasonable perspective or clearly see positive opportunities for change. Over time, social isolation compounds and exacerbates feelings of anger and frustration in a cycle that can lead to violence.

Economic Imperatives

Shifting employment opportunities. Most Americans are quite aware of the significant changes that have impacted the national economy since the end of World War II. America has moved away from its long-established base of industrial employment opportunities to become a nation that relies on technology, electronics, and information exchange. The American economy has been the beneficiary of several decades of incredible technological innovation, which has transformed the lives of most citizens. The benefits of this technology are clear; the disadvantages are to be expected. As this nation continues to generate new employment opportunities in technology-related areas, old ways of working are being abandoned. Unfortunately, many employees are unable to make a successful transition from the established employment opportunities of the past to the new opportunities of the future. The result of this pervasive change is to obviate established skills, and entire careers, in order to purse new horizons.

Middle-age employees are most impacted by significantly shifting employment opportunities. These employees may have spent much of their lives learning a skill or trade that is suddenly made obsolete or less important due to technological change. At times, entire organizations or industry segments become displaced by technological change, which can represent an economic and social threat to mid-career employees who find their future options limited. Without a great deal of personal assistance for employees experiencing a significant life transition brought on by technological change, a worker may feel abandoned, frustrated, and angry. It is an unfortunate fact that most organizations lack the capacity or inclination to devote the resources necessary to enable a worker displaced by technological change to reestablish his economic and social worth. Without adequate support for positive change, this kind of significant life displacement can, in some workers, trigger aggressive and violent reactions.

Abandonment of commitment. There has been a significant erosion in the depth of commitment between an employer and employee over the past few decades. For a variety of reasons, including worker mobility, economic shifting, changing work environments, and fierce competition, the expected bond between a worker and his or her organization is often surprisingly weak. Employees are frequently distrustful of their employers and quick to point out that organizational loyalty to workers is regularly sacrificed for short-term profitability. Similarly, many corporate managers feel that their employees are not truly committed to the organization and would quickly leave for greener pastures. In fact, there is much truth to both positions. Today, the bond between employee and employer is not a strong one, despite the expectation of loyalty that was prevalent a few decades ago when many of today's long-term employees first entered the workforce. This is a point of disillusionment and frustration for many workers and organizational managers.

Middle-age employees who have worked for the same organization for several years or decades often believe they have a right to expect a high degree of employer loyalty. They view their contributions as significant and their worth to their employer as high. These same workers, however, may be viewed quite differently by the employer. Organizational managers may perceive the long-term employee as especially costly in terms of salary and benefits. This worker may be seen as unable to progress in a changing work environment or lacking in current skills. Perhaps he or she is viewed as inflexible or unwilling to adapt to new technologies or too expensive to retrain. Whatever the reason, it is not uncommon for the employee's perception of his services to be quite different than his employer's. Where the employee finds himself loyal and experienced, the employer might perceive unnecessary expense and inflexibility. With such naturally divergent views, it is possible that a violent misunderstanding could result from any significant change in organizational strategy that threatens a worker with potential job loss.

Whenever possible, organizations should make considerable efforts to integrate their existing workforce into any reorganization strategy. The tempting expediency to eliminate long-term workers simply because they represent a high per-employee cost base is both short-sighted and dangerous. There are many alternatives to eliminating these workers which, in the end, could better achieve the organization's goals while maintaining an essential degree of employee trust and loyalty. From the point of view of a violence prevention program, the significant divergence in perceptions of employee value cannot be disregarded as a contributor to violence. Employees *are* valuable and should never be regarded as only of consequence from a bottom-line perspective. To devalue the worth of a worker in this way and treat him accordingly is to invite anger and potential retribution into the workplace.

Corporate profit wars—Downsizing and layoffs. For the past two decades, American corporations have engaged in a frenzy of mergers, acquisitions, and trades. Major conglomerates were formed, while others were dissolved or abandoned. New industries have arisen in response to astounding technological innovations in the areas of electronics, software, and communications. Established corporations have fallen victim to these same innovations, suffering significant economic losses or undergoing pervasive restructuring. Government regulations have created new organizational structures; they have rewarded competition and, at times, stifled it. The era of corporate profit wars has been well underway for some time in America, and much more so than has ever before been experienced in our history.

The shifting and struggling of organizations in an effort to maintain or increase profits invariably impacts employees significantly. For most corporations, the cost of their human resources is significant. When the dynamics of organizational profitability come into play and cost-reduction measures are deemed to be the order of the day, reducing the company employee base will most often provide a quick and effective solution. In other circumstances, an organization will elect to *downsize*: to recreate itself in a new, lean form that can affect profits in a positive way. Whatever the rationale or method, the expense category of choice will often be the employee base—and typically, the largest drain on organizational profits. In the past two decades, it has become almost fashionable for an organization to invoke the concepts of downsizing or layoffs in an effort to secure short-term profitability. In less fortunate situations, corporations have been left without other options.

Regardless of the reason, the elimination of employees by any method can be catastrophic. When reducing their employee base, organizations will often target high-cost employees—those who may have been with the organization for some time and are more costly in terms of compensation than entry-level workers. Particularly vulnerable are middle managers, whose responsibilities may be consolidated or eliminated entirely with organizational shifting. Many middle-aged, male workers, with significant organizational histories and compensation to match, may be viewed as unnecessarily expensive in the context of a reorganization plan. Unfortunately, these same workers may desperately need to maintain their jobs and are least likely to easily reenter the workforce.

Workers who have perfected only a single skill, which then becomes unnecessary, are also highly vulnerable to organizational shifting. These employees may become the victims of technology or changing economic markets with little or no warning. They experience the anguish of possessing a skill—perhaps one perfected over a lifetime—that is no longer marketable. In many situations, they are not provided with the opportunity to learn new skills or, if they do receive that opportunity, the results are disappointing when they make an effort to re-enter the workforce. In effect, these workers have been completely abandoned by the economics of the American workplace and have little likelihood of ever recapturing what they have lost.

Unemployment is a pervasive and escalating problem in this country, yet it is often disguised by a simple statistic—the percentage of the population who are unemployed. Although this is a valuable statistic, it is one which disregards the real impact of being without work in a society where a job is economically and socially crucial. The actual number of unemployed Americans is not only staggering, it represents a threat to the nation's economic and social welfare that has yet to be resolved.

The raw number of unemployed workers has nearly tripled since 1950 and continues to increase at an alarming rate (see Figure 3.3). Well over 8 million Americans are currently without work. They are subject to the same financial and social pressures as their employed neighbors or friends, but they cannot compete effectively in society or adequately support themselves or their dependents. Since 1970, the number of unemployed workers has doubled—amounting to millions of Americans impacted by two decades of organizational downsizing and layoffs. Many of these unemployed workers face overwhelming difficulties when trying to reenter the workforce; few will ever again attain the earning power or position they once could claim.

Figure 3.3: Numbers of Unemployed, 1950-1993 (Millions)[7]

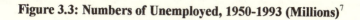
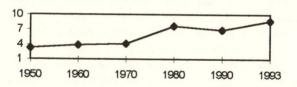

The fear of downsizing and layoffs is pervasive in many industries—and this fear is justified. Established, well-paid workers are frequently anxious about their futures, uncertain and unaware of organizational planning, and, perhaps, suspicious of the motives for sweeping corporate change. The male middle-aged worker, because of his relative high-cost factor or possession of only a single skill, is often the target of economic change, and he knows it. He is also aware that many organizations will make little or no effort to help him reenter the workforce after he loses his job. Aware of the vast number of unemployed workers, and understandably anxious about an impending and radical change in lifestyle and self-esteem, the employee facing termination may have grave concerns about his future. Given the significant changes in the American economy over the past two decades, his deep concerns may be quite valid.

The scenario of a male middle-aged worker facing the loss of his job has become increasingly common in recent years. It is a situation fraught with danger for both the employee and the employer. Incidents of workplace violence or homicide are often linked to the triggering event of a recent job loss, or even to the perceived threat of such a loss that has not yet actually occurred. Employees who have lost their jobs may react with sudden violence— sometimes with devastating impact upon the organization and former coworkers. They may also depart quietly and return, even as long as a year later, with lethal retribution in mind. The effect of a job loss upon any employee is not predictable. Much depends upon the individual and his ability to cope with the pernicious and sometimes lasting effects of unemployment.

Despite the increasing incidence of violence that plagues the American workplace because of downsizing and layoffs, many organizations pay little attention to the obvious prevention methodology of ensuring that terminated employees are capable of reentering the workforce as quickly as possible. Workers caught in any economic strategy that threatens their job or career may perceive their situation as desperate, with few remaining options. An organization which disregards this understandable reaction may be enabling an act of violence or homicide that could have been averted with planning and sensitivity.

Workplace Imperatives

Stress and the dangerous workplace. A poor work environment can become a breeding ground for violence; however, the quality of the work environment is a factor that is often considered only *after* incidents of violence or homicide occur. Questions have been raised about certain stressful types of work environments, such as those that exist at the U.S. Postal Service, and the enabling effect they may have on potentially violent or lethal employees. It is known from the behavioral sciences that long periods of stress can lead to aggressive or violent behavior. Given that millions of American workers spend at least eight hours each day, possibly for decades, in a single work environment, these surroundings clearly have a significant impact on a worker's perspective, expectations, attitude, and stress level. To the extent that the work environment provides a positive, enriching experience, the potential for violence is decreased. If the opposite is true, however, aggression and violence are enabled.

A work environment can suffer from any number of factors that introduce unnecessary stress among the workforce. There are certain elements known to induce stress, destroy a positive work environment, and increase the potential for violence. When evaluating the potential for violence presented by an employee, it is important to give consideration to the work environment that has helped to formulate his current attitude and perspective. Much of the frustration and anger exhibited by the potentially lethal employee may be attributable to factors within the work environment itself.

Of primary importance to employees are issues of *safety* and *general working conditions*. Workers must feel secure on the job and physically comfortable in the work environment. If the workplace invites physical danger or discomfort, and these issues are not immediately addressed, a significant level of stress will become apparent among the workforce. Continual subjection to the stress of an uncomfortable or unsafe work environment can not only quickly destroy the morale of an organization, it can lead to defensive, aggressive, and hostile behavior among employees.

Inept or uncaring management can create a working environment in which distrust is rampant and teamwork is negated or destroyed. Workers want to be appreciated by their supervisors, trusted, and treated with dignity and respect. If workers feel misused or victimized by management, a barrier will be established that can quickly polarize work groups and disrupt or destroy lines of communication. This is an issue that must be addressed by workplace managers on a continual basis. It is their responsibility to deal with workers honestly, fairly, and in an open manner. Critical to this relationship is the supervisor's commitment to keeping employees informed of any matter that affects them or the work environment.

Inadequate rewards for work will induce frustration and anger among the workforce. This is a matter of both compensation (salary and benefits) and recognition. Workers must feel that they are fairly compensated for their work and recognized for their accomplishments. Compensation packages must be on a par with relative industry standards in order to attract and maintain an effective workforce. Of primary consideration is the sufficiency of benefit programs for workers—an issue that is often critical to the wellness of an employee and his or her family. In addition, an organization should be sensitive to the needs of workers to be recognized publicly for their accomplishments. The bond of trust that is necessary to promote a nonviolent workplace is made strong by supervisors who adequately compensate and regularly recognize the achievements of their workers. Disregarding these elements can easily produce feelings of frustration and anger in the workforce—the precursors of violent behavior.

Ineffective training and education programs can lead to an array of stressors in the workplace such as increased industrial accidents, worker stagnation, the elimination of in-house promotional opportunities, intellectual stagnation, and a generally less effective workforce. When employees are provided with the opportunity to enhance their skills or education, both the organization and the worker benefit in obvious ways. It is vital to the sense of well-being for workers that they perceive the workplace as always providing opportunity. This does not imply the necessity for upward career mobility across each job category. Rather, and more appropriately, it implies a willingness on the part of the employer to assist the worker to improve his skills and become better at what he does. Quality work is a source of pride for most employees; it is an issue that can bind the employee and employer in a relationship of mutual respect and teamwork. An organization whose management is perceived by workers as concerned about all staff and willing to assist them enhance their skills and education will generate significantly increased worker loyalty, and thereby decrease the likelihood of workplace violence.

Inadequate communication fosters misunderstanding, hostility, and violence. Communication across all segments of an organization must be open and strong in order to foster the concept of nonviolence at work. When individuals are cut off from each other or fail to communicate across group lines, the opportunities for misunderstanding, which leads to aggression, are multiplied. However, if management vigorously endorses open communication among all employees and itself sets the example, individual workers tend to form more meaningful relationships and are less likely to address coworkers or supervisors with aggression.

The essential nature of open communication is especially critical during times of *organizational change*, which is inherently stressful for all workers, especially if they are not informed or informed inadequately. Whenever change disrupts the work environment, it has the potential to impact individual workers significantly. Employees will experience less frustration and react with less aggression if they are informed of issues that may impact the work environment and provided information about how such change will affect them personally.

Psychological Imperatives

There are numerous well-established psychological imperatives for violence. Long periods of frustration, stress, depressive states, and certain personality disorders, (such as antisocial personality disorder) are often linked with aggression and violence. Singular, traumatizing occurrences, such as separation from a partner, the death of a loved one, or the loss of a job, can operate as psychological triggering events for violence. Delusional disorders, fixations, or an obsession with another individual can also lead to aggressive behavior.

The lethal employee is often plagued with deep frustrations over a significant period of time. The individual who murders his supervisors or coworkers does not commit to such a heinous crime on the spur of the moment. Rather, the process that culminates in murder, particularly if there are multiple victims, is typically a long one. The lethal employee will often be angered about a number of critical life issues and frustrated with a variety of life circumstances. He may threaten violence and mayhem for many years before acting it out in the workplace; indeed, he may never act it out at all. When he does commit the crime there will likely be a significant *triggering event* that can be identified. This triggering event will serve as the culmination of a long period of escalating anger and frustration with which the perpetrator can no longer cope. This is a common pattern of developing violence for the lethal employee—but it is by no means the only possible one.

An employee may become lethal because of a profound depression or, perhaps, a singular event not preceded by a chronic disorder; he may be the victim of a transitory psychological condition or fugue state, either previously undiagnosed or just at its onset. An employee may also react with extreme and unpredictable violence when intoxicated, under the influence of a variety of drugs, subjected to certain hazardous or toxic chemicals, or in a moment of uncontrolled rage brought on by any number of circumstances. A worker may murder without warning in response to domestic or personal triggering events not at all related to his job and unsuspected by his coworkers or supervisors. An act of violence or murder linked to any of these circumstances will be nearly impossible to predict and very difficult to prevent.

There are innumerable and complex psychological imperatives for violence which are inherent in American society. Some of these, such as certain well-understood personality disorders, can be useful in prevention because they constitute somewhat reliable predictors of potential violence. However, many, and perhaps most, psychological imperatives are not particularly useful as predictors of violence. The effects of stress and frustration are pervasive in American society, and the vast majority of workers handle these issues in a nonviolent way. Domestic relationships are often strained and difficult, but few rejected partners commit murder. Depression is a common psychological disorder in this country, but few who suffer from it kill others. Evidence of obvious psychological imperatives for violence are helpful only in combination with other behavioral warning signs; in and of themselves, these imperatives cannot be used as reliable predictors of violence. Far too many individuals are impacted by these imperatives yet remain able to successfully resolve critical personal or work issues in a peaceful manner. An understanding of these imperatives can, however, aid in prevention and intervention programs directed at addressing and defusing areas of frustration or assisting employees to cope with difficult personal or work issues before violence becomes an alternative.

The Disillusionment of a Generation

The American workforce is now significantly populated by children born in the late 1940s, 1950s, and early 1960s—an era that began with high expectations but fell short of its promise. These same workers are frequently disillusioned and frustrated with a number of critical life issues at work and at home. With many unresolved issues and a view of the future that is less bright than their remembrances of the past, some of these individuals will inevitably react with anger and violence.

Recurring periods of economic instability, sweeping industrial change, the introduction of highly sophisticated technology throughout the work environment, increasing worker mobility, the transformation of the traditional family structure, and an increase in workplace stressors have all combined to impact much of the current workforce. The expectations of many male middle-aged workers have not been realized; many are plagued with chronic frustration and an inability to achieve the satisfaction of a career that they felt was both earned and deserved. Millions of these workers have reached a point in their career where they are earning at, or near, the top of their pay scale, with little opportunity for meaningful future advancement. These same workers are threatened by recent waves of downsizing and layoffs as corporations continue to shift strategies in order to reduce costs or increase profits. Organized programs to retrain workers who have lost their jobs are often absent or ineffectual. Careers are threatened by the economics of the workplace, efforts at diversity, and the changing profile of the American worker as employment needs shift and change. To many, the questions of organizational survival and personal survival are one and the same; they are convinced that they simply could not go on should they lose their job. Work has become a fundamental question of survival and they see few alternatives to making every effort to keep what they have worked so hard and long to attain, even if they are dissatisfied with the work or the work environment. Although they may overtly subscribe to the concept of teamwork on the job, many are personally convinced that the work environment represents an arena for survival of the fittest, or the luckiest, and that their personal welfare is usually regarded as secondary. Sadly, this situation may be more prevalent than most organizational executives would be willing to admit.

Many of these same employees are also confronted with significant domestic stressors. Changing family roles, insufficient leisure time, housing expenses, and the rising costs of vital services create significant burdens for many. Failed personal relationships, the breakup of the family, and social isolation present challenges that are at best difficult, and sometimes overwhelming, for numerous workers. Increasingly, the workplace represents a vital forum for socialization for numerous workers who have been displaced from their families or lack other domestic support. The lives of many employees have become so focused upon their need for recognition and success in the work environment that their job may provide the sole point of self-esteem to which they can lay claim. In essence, their jobs have become their lives. For some, losing their job may not only result in financial ruin but also signify the end to any social support network whatsoever.

The number of American workers who have become disillusioned with the meaning and purpose of their careers is not known; however, few would argue against the belief that it is considerable. This disillusionment and frustration is common among male middle-aged workers and, perhaps, many other groups in the workforce. It is clearly pervasive in the ranks of the violent or lethal employee. It cannot be mere coincidence that the prototypical lethal employee, as with the majority of violent employees, so often exhibits high levels of frustration and disappointment with critical aspects of his life.

What has been said about the economic and social imperatives for violence should not be considered a condemnation of a generation of American workers. The number of employees who become violent is not great; fewer still become lethal. The vast majority of workers are able to deal with their disillusionments and frustrations in positive ways, moving consistently ahead as best they can. However, a decade of workplace violence and murder clearly indicates an increase in the number of workers who fail to cope with the stressors of a complex home and work life, and so lash out violently against their coworkers or others. Any effort at preventing workplace violence through threat assessment or the recognition of behavioral warning signs should not disregard the profound impact of the frustrations and disappointments that have affected millions of American workers in recent decades.

NOTES

1. Eugene D. Wheeler and S. Anthony Baron, *Violence in Our Schools, Hospitals and Public Places*, (Ventura, CA: Pathfinder, 1994), 154-155.

2. "New Study Warns of Risks of TV Violence." *Reuter's New Media*, Internet, 7 February 1996.

3. U.S. Department of Labor, Bureau of Labor Statistics, unpublished tabulations from *Current Population Survey*, 1993.

4. Ibid.

5. U. S. Department of Commerce, Bureau of the Census, *Microsoft Bookshelf*, 1995 ed., Redmond, WA.: Microsoft Corporation. Computer software.

6. Ibid.

7. Ibid.

4

Intervention and Prevention

Every time history repeats itself the price goes up.

—Anonymous

There is an element of irony and horror in this otherwise laughable quote. The history of crimes perpetrated by the lethal employee unequivocally demonstrates that we have not yet learned how to protect our workers or the workplace—the price is indeed rising, and at an alarming rate. In many ways, our national workforce has been abandoned to what is perceived to be an uncontrollable wave of violence in which over a thousand workers each year pay the ultimate price. Many of these men and women are slain by a coworker—by a lethal employee.

Despite the long history of this crime and its escalating impact upon the workforce, organizations are typically slow to embrace the issue and reluctant to do what is needed to turn back the tide of aggression and murder. Whether the argument is one of low statistical probability, lack of perceived resources, fear, or a general reluctance to deal with issues of potential liability, avoiding the challenge of dealing proactively with the problems presented by the potentially violent or lethal employee has the effect of enabling future violence. The lethal employee today holds the workplace hostage, and his partner may well be the organization itself—an organization that may have already succumbed to victimization by neglect, avoidance, or an ignorance of the issues.

The commitment to a truly nonviolent and safe workplace is not simple or inexpensive. It requires a vigorous philosophy of organizational wellness and a depth of sensitivity to staff that is rare in the American business community. It demands that two key concepts be given the highest organizational priority—

intervention and prevention. It can only be truly effective if the organizational commitment to nonviolence is unquestioned, complete, and pervasive throughout the workforce.

Despite the hardships and costs, in the final analysis, an organization may have no option but to pursue a rigorous and companywide course of nonviolence. Anything less may, in the future, be tantamount to a capitulation to violence and murder in a form that is devastating, unpredictable, and inevitable. Surely, the price of avoiding the critical transition to a workplace free of violence has already proven to be too high to be further ignored.

INTERVENTION

The process of intervention involving a potentially violent employee must be handled with care, commitment, credibility, and sensitivity. It is important to keep in mind that very few employees become lethal but those few will inevitably resort to violence if intervention is not forthcoming and effective. Attempting to predict who will become violent or lethal is unwise and often unsuccessful. A much better approach to intervention is one which is based on a concern for the affected employee, the workforce, and the ability of all parties to reach a successful conclusion to the problem at hand. It is a mistake to react defensively or to immediately consider punitive measures as a preemptive strategy.

It is vital to keep in mind that the potentially violent worker is probably not functioning in the most rationale or best manner and may require a great deal of support to ensure that violence does not occur. A worker who is exhibiting the warning signs of potential violence will be deeply involved in his own problems and generally suspicious of the motives of those around him. He may be angry, threatening, intimidating, withdrawn, or even incoherent; he will generally be unable to reach a high level of objectivity about either his actions or the motives of those around him. In order to effectively intervene with such a person it is first necessary to establish trust and reliable communications. Therefore, an important dynamic of any effort at intervention is to approach each situation as unique; avoid being unduly influenced by policies, procedures, or preconceived concepts. The individual who is the subject of intervention will require a great deal of attention, much of which must be unique and personal in nature if it is to be effective.

Ingredients for Successful Intervention

Time is of the essence. There is a natural reluctance by most individuals to confront difficult or potentially dangerous situations. However, when dealing with a potentially violent worker, time is usually not an ally. The employee who is frustrated, angry, or withdrawn will seek a resolution to his grievances quickly and may well believe that each day without resolution only compounds his plight. Even if it is impossible to begin the intervention process immediately (which is ideal), the affected worker should know that his concerns are shared by others and will be addressed quickly. For organizations subject to rigid and cumbersome personnel policies, such as many governmental agencies, matters must not be left to run their course in a bureaucratic, impersonal manner. Ponderous and insensitive responses to an employee who is in difficulty will only exacerbate his frustrations and provide convincing evidence that his situation has not been given reasonable priority. Obviously, it is unwise to ignore well-designed personnel practices and policies; however, a sensitive and effective approach to intervention dictates that, at a minimum, some immediate assessment of the affected worker's condition be made, and, from that, assistance must be provided by a counselor, mental health professional, or employee assistance program. To simply ignore the growing signs of aggression, frustration, or potential violence exhibited by an employee is a sure way to rapidly worsen a deteriorating situation.

Have adequate resources available. When addressing the problems presented by a potentially violent employee, it is important to assemble an interdisciplinary team. Issues of employee rights, safety, security, privacy, and the law must all be considered in any intervention effort. At a minimum, the intervention team should be comprised of a mental health professional or representative from an employee assistance program, a human resources specialist, a legal representative, a security or safety representative, and a member of the organization's senior management. In an ideal situation, a threat assessment specialist or staff psychologist would also be included. It is foolhardy to attempt to intervene with a potentially violent employee unless these resources are available. Simply dealing with the complexities of employee rights and the law demands a teamwork approach in order to minimize liability. Beyond this, many potentially lethal employees are suffering from significant psychological problems that require the attendance of a mental health professional.

Know the employee's history and background. Members of the intervention team and, in particular, the individual assigned to interact with the potentially violent employee must be familiar with the employee's work history and background. An angered and frustrated employee who is on the verge of violence may quickly and aggressively react to otherwise insignificant stimuli. It is imperative that any individual who is attempting to intervene with the employee know and understand his background, history, and, to every extent possible, apparent motivations. The process of intervention demands that the potentially violent employee be addressed in a sensitive, personal manner to indicate that his value as an individual is recognized and appreciated. This approach can only be successful if the members of the intervention team are as familiar as possible with the employee. Preparation such as reviewing personnel files and interviewing coworkers is essential to successful intervention. The more that is known and understood about the potentially violent employee, the greater the likelihood of successful intervention.

Understand recent events and circumstances. It is vital to look for triggering events. Typically, the potentially violent employee will have experienced one or more identifiable triggering events that have pushed him to his current crisis. Often, due to a long period of anger and frustration, the most recent triggering event may seem relatively insignificant or easily overcome to an individual not caught up in the crisis of the moment. It must be remembered, though, that the frustrated and angered worker is unable to deal with such events in an objective, dispassionate manner. Whether the triggering event is related to the work environment, as with the possibility of a job loss, or personal, such as separation from a loved one, the affected employee may view the organization or specific workplace personnel as responsible for one or more events that have led to his present situation. The individual interviewing a potentially violent employee must be aware of this possibility and prepared to work toward an understanding of any triggering event.

Triggering events often seem overwhelming to the potentially violent employee. They may be perceived as insurmountable obstacles that allow for no options but retaliation or revenge. It is important that any triggering event be recognized for its impact on the individual and dealt with as crucial to the intervention process. When dealing with the employee, these events should never be diminished or made to appear insignificant. Rather, they must be understood and approached with sensitivity and objectivity.

Focus on intervention, not procedure or punishment. A potentially violent employee should not be the object of unthinking retribution or insensitive personnel policies used as the sole measure of intervention. However, this is not to say that personnel policies should be disregarded for the sake of expediency or perceived safety. If an employee violates important policies, and in doing so endangers coworkers or the workplace, it is imperative that action be taken to maintain order in the organization. However, the first order of business is to defuse the potentially violent situation and protect the work environment. The aggressive or hostile actions of a potentially violent employee cannot be tolerated in the workplace, yet in the midst of a crisis situation, the primary objective should be to stabilize the situation, not to enforce policies.

It is imperative that any intervention attempt focus upon minimizing the threat to others and stabilizing the current situation. This will often mean that any question of a policy violation must be temporarily put aside until the potentially violent situation has been defused and control reestablished. Many crimes committed by lethal employees have developed out of the added complications brought on by a cycle of employer actions based on policy enforcement followed by growing aggression on the part of the employee. There is a time and place for policy issues and employee disciplinary measures, but only after a potentially violent situation has been stabilized.

Be nonthreatening yet firm and committed. It is foolhardy to threaten an individual who is himself threatening violence. The potentially violent employee will often perceive the actions of others as threatening to himself, even when such actions are not intended to have this effect. When interacting with an angered and frustrated employee, it is imperative that he not feel intimidated or criticized. Any conversation with the employee must be honest, sensitive, and direct. The potentially violent employee must never feel that he is being manipulated or pressured, but rather, that he is receiving the full attention of the interviewer, who is genuinely interested in resolving the current crisis.

Make no commitment you cannot keep—Establish trust and credibility. The potentially violent employee is often distrustful of coworkers and supervisors, and perhaps of the entire organization. Therefore, any process of intervention must be undertaken with the highest standards of honesty and trust in mind. If the employee is to be helped and the workplace made safe, all communications must be credible. The interviewer should never deceive the angered employee or undertake any commitment that cannot be fulfilled. Credibility should be established in small ways so that the affected employee comes to understand and trust the interviewer's motivations. Once trust is established with the employee, it is usually possible to mutually work toward a resolution of the crisis and establish control over the situation.

Work to resolve or ameliorate critical issues first. It is imperative to know and understand the issues most critical to the potentially violent employee. The affected worker may have a number of problems that have combined to induce his current state of crisis. Once communication lines have been opened and trust has been established, it is important to focus on the issues that are most crucial to the employee. To the extent that some resolution can be reached regarding the critical issues, it may be possible to concurrently diminish the negative impact of the secondary issues. The employer must work with the affected employee to identify and understand the most important issues first and, if possible, should join with the individual to seek ways to defuse, ameliorate, or eliminate these primary causal factors.

Be persistent and supportive but not intrusive. Many potentially violent employees, especially if they are in a crisis state, may try to avoid efforts to intervene and assist. Be persistent in offering support and intervention, but do not threaten or push the issue. It is important that the affected worker understand that the organization is truly interested in helping to resolve the current crisis, but that it is equally vital the individual want that assistance. If the potentially violent employee rejects initial offers of assistance, find alternative ways to present this option to him. In the end, it may be necessary to let the worker know that intervention is required if he is to avoid disciplinary action; however, this should be a last resort. It is much more effective to guide the employee to an awareness of his options and have him join with the organization in resolving the current situation.

Use proper conduct in the interview. When conducting an interview with a potentially violent employee, proper conduct can make the difference between defusing a critical situation and making it more volatile. Any interaction with an employee in crisis must be handled with great care, sensitivity, and courage. The interviewer's demeanor must be calm and professional; quick or volatile motions or hand gestures must be avoided, and the employee must be addressed in a confident, nonthreatening tone. Critical to the success of any intervention attempt is the interviewer's ability to listen: it is imperative not to attempt to take initial control of the situation by interjecting unnecessary comments or conversation. The affected employee must be allowed to fully express his feelings and describe his circumstances. The interviewer must therefore listen with great attention and let the employee know that he or she is willing to do so until all of the facts are heard. Since such a conversation is often laced with emotion, it is imperative that the interviewer acknowledge the emotional content of the conversation, remain empathetic, but not be swayed from the primary objective of defusing the situation and mutually resolving the most critical issues.

It is important that the interviewer work to calm the environment yet not trivialize any comments made by the potentially violent employee. The most successful interviewer will work toward small points of understanding and agreement as the basis for calming the situation, always attempting to improve communications and establish trust. This may often mean that the interviewer must endure an initial onslaught of criticism and hostility. It is important to allow the employee to work through this initial period of aggression unimpeded, so long as the situation does not devolve into violence.

When the employee has achieved a state in which he can begin to address issues, it is time to work toward mutual resolution. During this phase it is important to help the employee understand that the issues *can* be resolved and are best approached by taking small steps leading to a larger resolution. At this point in the conversation, it is possible to introduce intervention measures designed to assist the affected employee, stabilize the crisis, and restore the work environment.

Follow up to resolve long-term issues. After intervention has taken place, and the potentially violent employee has responded favorably, do not assume that the matter is resolved. The issues that drive individuals to violent reactions can resurface or appear to be resolved when they are not. It is important to follow up with the affected employee to ensure that the intervention process has truly been effective and that no secondary issues have arisen that could result in a repeat of the crisis situation. In addition, such follow-up is typically appreciated by the individual and recognized as an indication that the organization is truly concerned about his welfare.

PREVENTION

Efforts designed to prevent violence or homicide in the workplace require a comprehensive commitment by all members of an organization. It is both unproductive and dangerous to give such a serious and pervasive issue only token attention without a comprehensive understanding of its impact and implications. Regardless of the safeguards in place within an organization, it is likely that some workers will, in one form or another, eventually threaten the security of the workplace. The disconcerting fact that violence can strike any organization at any time must be accepted and understood by both staff and management. Unwelcome as the prospect may be, workplace violence perpetrated by an employee or ex-employee threatens an ever-increasing number of workers annually in a wide variety of jobs and locations. The only effective line of defense against violence that threatens the workplace is the staff and management of the organization.

The epidemic of violent crime that so significantly affects the American workforce from within can be addressed by most organizations if the possibilities of workplace violence are recognized—not avoided—and all members of the staff join together in a comprehensive prevention program. The actions of the violent employee can be minimized; his crimes may, in some cases, be avoidable. As many of the case studies in this book have shown, there are often opportunities for intervention before a violent crime is committed by an employee or ex-employee. The key is to recognize these opportunities and be prepared to intervene quickly and effectively before violence or murder becomes inevitable.

The most fundamental form of violence prevention is to create a work environment in which the possibility of violence is minimized or excluded. This is obvious, but it is certainly not a clear and simple undertaking. Violence is prevalent in American society, and it is simply not possible to isolate the workplace or the workforce of any organization from the many imperatives that lead an individual to resort to aggression. It is possible, however, to vastly improve the safety and security of most work environments through a proactive commitment to nonviolence. This implies an organizational structure and philosophy that emphasizes the worth of the individual, recognizes the importance of communications, and encourages mutual respect and a deep interest in the wellness of each member of the staff—concepts that are subject to ready consensus yet are often missing in the work environment.

The most effective deterrent to violence or homicide in the workplace is a multifaceted approach that emphasizes several broad areas of philosophical and financial commitment:

1. *The organization must be committed to a proactive program of nonviolence in the workplace and must support this commitment financially.* Crucial prevention resources such as employee assistance programs, counseling, access to mental health professionals or support networks, wellness programs, education, training, and a strong human resources program must be vigorously supported by management, adequately funded, and accessible to all staff.

2. *Employees throughout the organization must be aware of the warning signs of potential violence and have at their disposal the means to quickly start the intervention process.* Staff must view the prevention of violence as a high priority and understand that all workers share equally in the safety of the workplace and the wellness of their coworkers.

3. *Organizational communications must be open across all lines so that vital information about critical workplace events is shared and acted upon in a teamwork environment before violence becomes inevitable.* Workers must be perceived as individually important, unique, and deserving of support in times of crisis, whether the challenges they encounter are on the job or elsewhere.

4. *Organizational management must be sensitive and open in their dealings with staff.* There must be an obvious and strong commitment by management to the welfare of the employees and the workplace. Credible, proactive leadership is essential to workplace security. It must be clear to each member of the staff that he or she is vital to the organization. The philosophy of the organization must insist on the highest standards of employee qualifications and conduct and, in return, provide the highest standard of employer commitment to staff.

5. *The organization must insist on a zero tolerance, intervention-oriented approach to employee harassment, hostility, and aggression.* Any behavior that is escalating toward violence or homicide must be quickly recognized and made the object of effective, team-oriented intervention.

6. *The organization must have clear goals that involve all staff and benefit both the workforce and the organization itself.* It is simply not sufficient to discuss the abstract concept of teamwork; it must become a reality in the workplace if violence is to be avoided. A worker who is concerned about, and committed to, the success of his coworkers is much less likely to act out violently than an individual who is forgotten, isolated, or not perceived as part of the team.

Within the structure of any organization there are key functions and activities that provide opportunities for increased workplace protection against the violent or lethal employee. Often, these activities are perceived as routine and not crucial to the establishment of a nonviolent workplace; however, they each provide areas of opportunity to improve the security of the work environment and move closer to the ideal goal of a completely nonviolent organization.

1. The *employment process* is crucial to establishing a nonviolent work environment. Employment activities are directly critical to the health of any organization and indirectly critical to every member of the workforce. If the process of employing an individual is weak or its importance is underrated by management, there is an increased possibility for eventual workplace violence through the introduction of inappropriate staff. On the other hand, a professional and effective employment process can do much to reduce the likelihood of hiring an individual who will later jeopardize the work environment. It should be obvious that the best and most effective method for preventing workplace violence and murder is to avoid hiring the potentially violent individual in the first place. This is a tall order, which may not be attainable in every organization all the time. It is possible, though, for most organizations to minimize the risks of violence through a vigorous and professional employment program that views violence prevention as an organizational priority and staffs its human resources department accordingly.

In many organizations the employment process is viewed as a lengthy, routine, staff-intensive burden of procedure and paperwork. Habits born of an inadequate understanding of legislation or the routine processing of applicants can lead to employment activities that are perceived as far less crucial to the wellness of the organization than they really are. Interviews may be overly scripted, superficial, unidirectional, uninformative, or not given the time and attention they deserve; background screening may be cursory or ineffective; the proper fit of applicant to organization or job may be ignored. The possible points of failure in the employment process are many and the opportunity to open the door to a potentially violent or lethal employee is always present. Despite its obvious importance, the employment process in many organizations is perfunctory and not supported with the highly skilled individuals and adequate funding it deserves.

2.   The *employee counseling process* can enable violence by establishing triggering events for retaliation, or it can ensure that potential violence is averted. Employee counseling is typically viewed as an activity reserved for the correction of work-related performance deficiencies or behavioral difficulties that are impacting the work environment. In this sense, it is frequently viewed as negative intervention—something to be avoided by management and staff if at all possible. However, a broader view of the employee counseling process embraces the concept of a positive intervention process—teamwork-oriented intervention that attempts to assist an employee who may be facing challenges on the job or elsewhere but who has not yet exhibited significant performance or behavioral problems. This is not to say that an employer should establish an organizationwide counseling program to deal with a limitless variety of personal, as well as personnel, problems presented by staff. Such an undertaking would be extreme and inappropriate. A middle-ground approach would dictate that the employer be concerned about employee wellness to the extent that the developing indications of a worker in difficulty are recognized and positive intervention is offered in the spirit of working toward a better workplace environment for all staff.

If an organization has the capability to intervene in a positive way before an employee experiences work performance or behavioral difficulties, the possibilities for violence are greatly reduced. Such a program of positive intervention must encompass strict confidentiality, an assistance-oriented approach, an attitude that focuses on the welfare of the affected individual, an understanding of his role in the organization, and the welfare of the general workforce. Ideally, such a program would be available directly to workers as well as by the referral of a coworker or supervisor. The program must also be perceived as offering genuinely positive intervention and as not imposing the traditional, more negative encounter commonly called "employee counseling."

3.   Like employee counseling, the *termination process* is fraught with danger and can contribute to violence or help in its prevention. As evidenced by many

cases of occupational homicide, there are few triggering events as pernicious or inherently dangerous as the termination of an employee. This is particularly true if the employee is over the age of thirty years, has a significant history with the organization, or has performed in the same skill category for many years. If the employee has reached middle age at the time of the termination (say over forty years), the possibility of a violent reaction increases significantly. When faced with a job loss, employees in this age category, especially those who have a significant history with the organization or who occupy responsible positions, are particularly vulnerable to a major disruption in their lives. They realize that the prospects for regaining what has been lost with their job are not good; they are acutely aware of the difficult financial and social transitions that follow in the wake of losing their job. A few individuals will perceive that the loss of their job represents an insurmountable challenge allowing no option but revenge. If an employee facing termination is already angered, frustrated, subject to social isolation, exhibiting significant behavioral problems, or confronting other difficulties in his life at the time of the termination, the loss of a job can present an irresistible triggering event for violence.

The termination of an employee should always be the last resort for any organization; it is not an activity that should ever be undertaken lightly or without deep consideration of its effect upon the individual and the workforce. It is a decision that must be subject to review by organizational experts in the areas of human resources, legal affairs, security, and senior management. The decision to discharge an employee must not be made in haste or anger but always in an objective and fair manner. Such a process should require multiple concurring opinions from members of the organization who understand the importance of their action, have carefully weighed their decision, and are sensitive to the implications of the termination for the individual and remaining staff.

If, after group consideration, the only option is termination, an important goal of the process should be to assist the departing employee to reenter the workforce as soon as possible. The loss of financial stability, dignity, social support, and perceived self-worth will significantly impact any departing employee, who will often be angry, resentful, and afraid. To simply discharge an individual who is facing these stressors, without regard to his future direction, is a dangerous and uncaring practice. On the other hand, making a genuine and reasonable effort to assist the departing employee to regain what he has lost can not only defuse a potentially violent situation but indicates to all staff that the organization will only undertake a termination as a last resort, and even then will not completely abandon the individual with the delivery of his final paycheck.

The way in which the termination process is undertaken is crucial to avoiding potential violence. The termination must be handled with dignity, professionalism, sensitivity, and respect. Issues must be clarified, and the individual's rights and concerns must be addressed with honesty. The timing of the termination is also critical. If at all possible, an employee should never be discharged when he or she is undergoing other stressful life situations such as the separation from a loved one or the death of a friend or family member. It should be expected that the discharged individual will react emotionally and, perhaps, with anger. It is important that the departing employee be given an opportunity to work through these emotions and, as necessary, be supported with follow-up counseling or employee assistance. If considered necessary, it may be prudent to have a member of the security staff present at any termination meeting. It is always a good practice to have two members of management present, one of whom is a human resources professional.

Of utmost importance to the termination process is to provide some meaningful support for re-entry into the workforce. Whether this be by way of an outplacement service, counseling, skill enhancement, training, or support services for locating a new job, it is imperative that the departing employee not feel completely abandoned. If provided with sufficient support, most employees who are terminated from their jobs can come to accept the situation and adapt to the significant changes that inevitably follow. It is in the best interests of the organization to participate actively in this need for support for a reasonable period of time after the employee departs.

4. *Staff education and training* are critical to the development of an involved, concerned, nonviolent workforce. It is generally recognized that an informed, highly skilled, and well-trained workforce not only benefits the organization but is less likely to experience aggression or violence within their ranks. It is equally important to train staff to recognize potentially violent situations and have available the tools necessary to effect speedy intervention when violence is a possibility.

It is clear that the subject of homicide by a coworker will never be a welcome issue in the workplace. This is a fundamentally disturbing topic which many workers would rather not discuss or ponder. Nonetheless, it is impossible to prevent workplace violence if the subject is avoided or only given cursory attention. The safety of the workplace demands that each worker not only be committed to a personal philosophy of nonviolence but be willing and able to recognize the potential for violence when it becomes apparent. As unsettling as the prospect may be, it is essential that the workforce be made aware of the possibilities of violence and understand how to best cope with it. Without such an understanding of the issue, it is impossible to implement a truly effective prevention program in any organization.

To achieve a high standard of organizational protection from the potentially violent worker, each member of the staff must know how to recognize the warning signs of escalating aggression. They must also have the confidence in management to know that any reasonable effort they make to protect the work environment will be taken seriously, held in confidence, and supported with appropriate intervention efforts. Achieving this level of trust among members of the workforce is not a simple matter, and it cannot be quickly attained. It implies a consistent demonstration by management, through their actions, that violence will not be tolerated—that employees who are exhibiting the warning signs of potential violence will receive positive intervention, not retaliation.

5.   *Organizational safety and security* programs define a commitment to nonviolence and provide forums for the exchange of information vital to the violence intervention process. Protecting the workforce from employee-perpetrated violence cannot be a top-down effort. True violence prevention is born of an individual commitment to safety, wellness, and nonviolence. Achieving such a consensus among members of the workforce is best realized when the staff is deeply involved in the process of safety and prevention. Safety and security teams derived from the workforce itself provide an excellent vehicle for averting potential violence. Members of the workforce who are involved in these teams are often highly regarded by their peers and trusted by their coworkers. They may have access to the workforce that is often denied to management personnel and therefore be among the first members of the organization to be aware of a developing, potentially violent situation. If the safety or security committee is properly staffed, provided with strong management support, and given the tools to implement prevention techniques in the workplace, they will often prove to be an excellent deterrent to violence.

A high level of awareness among staff regarding the implications of workplace violence can also be achieved by safety or security personnel who are members of the workforce and have the ear and respect of their coworkers. They provide an effective and valued resource for education, information, and training for other staff members. Such committees can also provide a mechanism to assess developing situations and arrange for professional, positive intervention that will be accepted by coworkers as evidence of a proactive, positive approach to personnel issues.

6.   *Communication* is crucial to a stable work environment; it is also the cornerstone of early intervention. When the crimes of many lethal employees are carefully analyzed it is common to find that coworkers were concerned about the possibility of violence before it occurred because they recognized one or more behavioral warning signs but were unable or unwilling to become involved. Coworkers are generally quite aware of the personalities and behavior patterns of their colleagues and they are typically the first to recognize that behavior has changed or their coworker is in some difficulty. Often, however, the individual who senses a developing situation does not understand the meaning of behavioral warning signs or is unable to arrange for assistance or intervention.

Workers are understandably reluctant to become involved in a delicate or potentially dangerous situation involving a coworker. Dealing with such a situation implies the involvement of management, with support by professionals as needed. The staff must, however, feel that they can report potentially dangerous situations to management in a way that ensures confidentiality and support. This presents a dilemma in most organizations—a decision whether to risk embarrassment or retaliation by reporting a situation to management or simply ignoring the warning signs and hope the problem will resolve itself. At the heart of this dilemma is the issue of communication.

If management is truly committed to a nonviolent workplace, it is fundamental that communications throughout the organization be comprehensive, open, and honest. To the extent that an organization is able to open all lines of communication from top to bottom, it is able to improve the opportunities for defusing violence. This means that mechanisms must be in place to ensure the protection and confidentiality of any employee who expresses concern about potential violence. It also demands that once the information is known to management, appropriate intervention occurs in a timely manner. The staff must be convinced that efforts to protect the workforce from an errant employee will be handled with discretion and a proactive, positive response.

7.   A forward-looking, *committed management team* is essential to the health of the organization. The management team of an organization sets a philosophy and tone that pervades the entire workforce. An uncaring, insensitive management team will not benefit from an involved, committed, and productive workforce. Indeed, a management team oriented toward an overbearing, intimidating style of supervision can expect to be victimized by workplace violence. On the other hand, managers who are positive, proactive, and involved with staff will earn respect and trust; they will, by their daily efforts, foster cooperation and nonviolence among the staff they supervise.

It is essential that supervisors and managers view each member of the workforce as an important individual whose true worth far exceeds his or her perceived value to the organization. The natural barrier that exists between management and staff does not imply a difference in personal value or worth, but rather, a difference in responsibility. Without question, it is the responsibility of management to create a work environment in which respect, honesty, and cooperation are essential elements. Managers must not only be sensitive to the ever-changing challenges confronted by the workforce but also highly skilled in problem solving and conflict resolution, always seeking an outcome that mutually benefits the employee *and* the organization. An attitude that implies that the value of the organization outweighs that of the individual worker fosters anger, frustration, and potential violence, while a management style that honors individual worth, values training, encourages self-improvement, and recognizes achievement fosters trust, respect, and nonviolent resolutions to problematic issues that arise in the workplace.

8.   An intervention team or *crisis management team* is a potent and effective defense against workplace violence and the lethal employee. Larger organizations are particularly vulnerable to workplace violence due to the number and diversity of staff and the inevitable turnover of personnel. An

intervention or crisis management team can provide the ability to respond quickly to impending violence and allow for positive intervention to defuse escalating situations involving staff.

A crisis management team is most effective if several key elements are apparent in its structure and activities:

A.   *The team should be interdisciplinary in nature.* That is, members should represent management, security, human resources, legal, and employee assistance; and there should be an employee representative. In addition to the standing members of the team, relevant staff, such as supervisors or coworkers, should join with the group in specific intervention activities as needed to best reach a strategy for resolution.

B.   *The crisis management team should be empowered by senior management to undertake its responsibilities in an unimpeded fashion.* This means that the group should be provided with the resources from both within and outside the organization in order to address an escalating situation quickly and effectively. The ability to arrange for positive intervention with a minimum of bureaucracy is essential.

C.   *The team should provide regular reports and information to senior management, along with recommendations for improvements in the workplace.* It is vital that the activities of the crisis management team be known to the organization's senior management so that strategic decisions about how to avert future violence are enacted rapidly and effectively.

D.   *The team should be proactive.* The crisis management team must not simply wait for a crisis and then act to resolve the situation. Rather, the group should be actively involved in planning, training, and crisis simulations so that staff are aware of its role and able to use it as a practical resource.

Members of the crisis management team must be highly skilled, well-trained individuals who have a background in conflict resolution and are able to interact effectively with employees in crisis. Since most organizations will eventually be confronted with some form of employee violence, the resource of a crisis management team that is well prepared and able to move into action quickly can have a profound impact in defusing problematic situations or averting future violence.

9.   A *quality work environment* is essential to the safety and security of employees; a substandard work environment enables violence. Workers who are subjected to difficult, unsafe, unhealthy, or debilitating work environments are more likely to react with violence than employees who enjoy a pleasant, rewarding, and enriching workplace. Organizational management must pay strict attention to the working environment because it is known to have a profound impact on the attitude and productivity of workers. The American

worker spends a great deal of time in the workplace, and its impact is cumulative. An environment that induces persistent stress for any reason enables eventual violence in individuals who would otherwise never resort to aggression or hostility.

Employees who must tolerate an inferior work environment will often attempt to convey their concerns to supervisors or managers. It is vital that these concerns, if reasonable, be seriously considered. Even though an employee may not specifically recognize the debilitating effects of a substandard work environment, he or she will typically express concerns or frustrations that can be linked to the workplace. Management should make every effort to ensure that the work environment itself does not provide, over time, a breeding ground for frustration, anger and eventual violence.

10. A *commitment to nonviolence*, by every member of the staff, is the highest achievable goal of any prevention program. If any member of the workforce presents the potential for violence, all members of the staff are at risk. Each member of the staff must be committed to a nonviolent solution to the difficulties they inevitably encounter at home and on the job. The organization must proactively support this kind of problem solving and set an example of involvement and sensitivity that makes a nonviolent workplace possible. A philosophy that embraces the highest standards of workplace behavior, and therefore provides a substantially improved level of safety for all, should embrace these personal commitments:

A. *I care.* I care about my coworkers, supervisors, the management of the organization, and its clients. I will guard the safety and integrity of others, and ask that they do the same for me.
B. *I am committed.* I am committed to nonviolence, safety, honesty, and success for myself, my organization, and all its members.
C. *I will communicate.* I recognize that the free flow of communication across all levels of the organization is vital to every member of the group. I will do my part to keep those lines of communication open and effective. I will hear others, and ask that they also hear me.
D. *I will show respect.* I will respect myself and other individuals. I will seek peaceful solutions and treat others, always, in a nonviolent way. My actions affect others, and theirs affect me; therefore, I will show respect, always.
E. *I will progress.* I choose to learn and grow in ways that better myself, my family, my organization, and my society. I want my organization to help me achieve my goals, and I, in turn, will help the organization achieve its goals.

5

Conclusion

Violence does, in truth, recoil upon the violent, and the schemer falls into the pit which he digs for another.
— Sir Arthur Conan Doyle
The Adventures of Sherlock Holmes

It is ultimately impossible to ensure complete protection from the potentially violent or lethal employee. The possibilities for violence are virtually limitless; the motivations of the perpetrator are sometimes covert, complex, or perhaps even unconscious; they are always difficult to comprehend when innocent workers are slain without reason or warning. The precise moment in which the lethal employee will strike is impossible to predict; the validity and seriousness of his threats, if any are made, are usually uncertain and always open to debate. His actions may seem random, indiscriminate, symbolic, or incomprehensible; they may also be extremely well-planned, vicious, and precise. The lethal employee has many advantages when the time to strike arrives.

Incidents of murder carried out by an employee or ex-employee are usually unexpected by staff and almost always deeply horrifying. These crimes strike at the heart of the workplace and violate a trust of teamwork, which is a high goal for any organization. Such violence and murder are personalized, frightening in the extreme, sometimes indiscriminate, and always extremely disruptive to the organization. This is a category of crime that truly holds the American workplace hostage by victimizing its core component—the worker. Sadly, it is a crime on which this nation has cornered the market. America is, by far, the world's leader in the victimization and murder of its own workers by its own workers.

Despite the many obvious difficulties inherent in the complex issues surrounding occupational homicide perpetrated by the lethal employee, there are possibilities for prevention. The activities and behavioral patterns of the potentially lethal employee are gradually becoming better understood. Although the element of uncertainty that derives naturally from any attempt to understand human behavior remains an obstacle—and always will—some headway has been realized in recent years. We have come to understand many of the behavioral warning signs that are frequent indicators of violence. The knowledge of triggering events and the important role they play in pushing an individual toward violence is improving. There is a growing and encouraging awareness within many American organizations of the impact of workplace violence and occupational homicide. Government agencies such as the National Institute for Occupational Safety and Health (NIOSH), the Centers for Disease Control and Prevention (CDC), the U.S. Department of Justice (DOJ), and others offer a variety of programs that address aspects of workplace violence and occupational homicide. A number of private industry groups have been formed to deal with these issues, while other organizations have devoted their energies to such important subjects as posttrauma counseling and personal safety programs. In most organizations, the possibilities for implementing effective violence prevention programs are increasing.

Of critical importance to any prevention program is the ability to identify potentially violent or lethal situations as early in the escalation process as possible. As many of the case studies in this book have shown, it is a common scenario for a potentially violent situation to veer out of control because there was no intervention or the intervention process was initiated too late. An argument can be made that hindsight is perfect and allows for the infallible recognition of developing violence; however, this argument is only partially valid and denigrates the ability of the American workforce to learn how to protect itself. There clearly *are* identifiable behavioral warning signs that are frequently linked to violence and murder—characteristics that can be understood and identified. There *are* certain patterns to the crime of occupational homicide perpetrated by the lethal employee—patterns that can be recognized and used as the basis for training and prevention. The *are* triggering events and imperatives for violence that can be discerned and generally understood. All these elements are tools to aid in the prevention of workplace violence if we choose to make wise use of them through understanding and education.

It is an absolute truth that violence is often unpredictable. It is defeatism to assume that the acts of violence and murder that hold the American workplace hostage are wholly random and beyond our ability to address. To simply dismiss this category of crime as beyond our capacity to understand or prevent is to admit we are helpless victims, forever consigned to the role of hostage. Such an attitude is antithetical to the meaning of the American workplace and U.S. society. Without a willingness to address the complex issues presented by the violent or potentially lethal employee we are, in effect, enabling the destruction of the American workplace by accepting a role as hostage. This is surely not an acceptable course.

Appendix

VIOLENCE PREVENTION RESOURCES

Occupational Safety and Health Administration (OSHA)
1120 20th St. NW
Washington, DC 20036
Telephone (202) 219-8148

OSHA Consultation Services - California
CAL/OSHA Consultation Service
Telephone (415) 703-4050

Centers for Disease Control
1600 Clifton Road NE
Atlanta, GA 30333

National Institute of Occupational Safety and Health (NIOSH)
4676 Columbia Parkway
Cincinnati, OH 45226-1998
Telephone 1-800-35-NIOSH
Fax (513) 533-8573

NIOSH - Atlanta
1600 Clifton Road NE
Atlanta, CA 30333
Telephone (404) 639-3061

United States Department of Labor
200 Constitution Ave. NW
Washington, DC 20210

Scripps Center Quality Management, Inc.
(Crisis Management Services)
9747 Business Park Ave.
San Diego, CA 92131
Telephone (619) 566-3472

Crime Victims Research and Treatment Center
Medical University of South Carolina
151 Ashley Ave.
Charleston, SC 29425
Telephone (803) 792-2945

American Society for Industrial Security
1655 North Fort Myer Dr.
Arlington, VA 22209
Telephone (703) 522-5800

American Psychological Association
750 1st Street, NE
Washington, DC 20006

Society of Human Resources Management
606 N. Washington Street
Alexandria, VA 22314
Telephone (703) 548-3440

National Crime Prevention Council
1700 K Street, NW, Suite 618
Washington, DC 20006
Telephone (202) 466-6272

National Institute for Mental Health
5600 Fishers Lane
Rockville, MD 20857
Telephone (301) 496-4000

Public Health Service
(Department of Health and Human Services) Region I Office
Government Center, Room 1875
Boston, MA 02203
Telephone (617) 565-1439

DHHS Region IV Office
101 Marietta Tower, Suite 1106
Atlanta, GA 30323
Telephone (404) 331-2396

DHHS Region VIII Office
1185 Federal Building
1961 Stout Street
Denver, CO 80294
Telephone (303) 844-6166

NIOSH Educational Resource Center - California
Center for Occupational and Environmental Health
Richmond Field Station
1301 S. 46th Street, Building 102
Richmond, CA 94804
Telephone (510) 231-5645

Selected Bibliography

American Psychiatric Association, *Diagnostic and Statistical Manual of Mental Disorders* (*DSM IV*). 4th ed. Washington, D.C.: American Psychiatric Association, 1994.

Backman , R. *Violence and Theft in the Workplace.* U.S. Department of Justice, Bureau of Justice Statistics, 15 July 1994.

Baron, S. A. *Violence in the Workplace.* Ventura, Calif.: Pathfinder, 1993.

Baron, S. A., and Wheeler, E. D. *Violence in Our Schools, Hospitals and Public Places.* Ventura, Calif.: Pathfinder, 1994.

Bell, C. A. "Female Homicides in United States Workplaces, 1980-1985." *American Journal of Public Health,* 6 (1991): 729.

Bell, C. A., Stout, N. A., Bender, T. R., Conroy, C. S., Crouse, W. E., and Myers, J. R. "Fatal Occupational Injuries in the United States: 1980-1985. *Journal of the American Medical Association,* 22 (1991): 1047.

Boxer, P. A. "Assessment of Potential Violence in the Paranoid Worker." *Journal of Occupational Medicine,* 2 (1993): 127.

U.S. Department of Labor, Bureau of Labor Statistics. Unpublished tabulations from *Current Population Survey,* 1993.

Castillo, D. N., and Jenkins, E. L. "Industries and Occupations at High Risk for Work-Related Homicide." *Journal of Occupational Medicine,* 2 (1994): 125.

Cowan, John S. "Lessons from the Fabrikant File: A Report to the Board of Governors of Concordia University." Concordia University, (1 May 1994): 13.

Duncan, T. Stanley. "Death in the Office—Workplace Homicides." *Law Enforcement Bulletin,* 64, no. 4 (April 1995): 20-25.

Fox, J. A., and Levin, J. *Overkill: Mass Murder and Serial Killing Exposed.* New York: Plenum, 1994.

Goldman, H. H., ed. *Review of General Psychiatry.* Norwalk, Conn.: Appleton and Lange/Prentice Hall, 1988.

Gross, Linden. "Twisted Love: A Deadly Obsession." *Cosmopolitan,* 213, no. 1 (July 1992): 190.

Hales, T., Seligman, P. J., Newman, S. C., and Timbrook, C. L. "Occupational Injuries Due to Violence." *Journal of Occupational Medicine,* 6 (1988): 483.

Hanley, Robert. "Co-Workers Are Stunned: 'No, It Couldn't Be True'." *New York Times,* 23 March 1995, B7.

Holmes, R. M. *Profiling Violent Crimes: An Investigative Tool.* Newbury Park, Calif.: Sage, 1990.

Kelleher, M. D. *New Arenas for Violence: Occupational Homicide in the American Workplace.* Westport, Conn.: Praeger, 1996.

Levy, Clifford J. "Former Montclair Post Worker Charged with Killings in Robbery," *New York Times,* 23 March 1995, A1.

Mantell, M. *Ticking Bombs—Defusing Violence in the Workplace.* New York: Irwin, 1994.

McCune, J. "Companies Grapple with Workplace Violence." *Management Review,* 3 (1994): 52.

Smith, S. L. "Violence in the Workplace: A Cry for Help." *Occupational Hazards,* 1 October 1993.

Stockdale, J., and Phillips, C. "Physical Attack and Threatening Behavior." *Occupational Health,* August 1989, 212.

Thomas, J. L. "A Response to Occupational Violent Crime." *Risk Management,* June 1992, 27.

Thomas, J. L. "Occupational Violent Crime: Research on an Emerging Issue." *Journal of Safety Research,* 2 (1992): 55.

Trebilcock, Tim. "I Love You to Death." *Redbook,* 178, no. 5 (March 1992): 100.

United States Department of Commerce. Bureau of Commerce. *Microsoft Bookshelf,* 1995 ed., Redmond, WA: Microsoft, 1995. Computer software.

Unites States House of Representatives. Committee on Post Office and Civil Service. *A Post Office Tragedy: The Shooting at Royal Oak.* Washington, D.C.: U.S. Government Printing Office, 1992.

United States Department of Health and Human Services (USDHHS). *Fatal Injuries to Workers in the United States, 1980-1989: A Decade of Surveillance.* USDHHS/National Institute of Occupational Safety and Health, August 1993.

Windau, J. and Toscano, G. "Murder Inc. - Homicide in the American Workplace." *Business and Society Review,* 89 (1994): 58.

Index

About the Author

MICHAEL D. KELLEHER, currently Executive Deputy Director of the Marin County Housing Authority, has held executive management positions in both the public and private sectors for 25 years. Throughout his career, Kelleher has specialized in strategic management, staff education, and crisis management and resolution. He is the author of *New Arenas for Violence: Homicide in the American Workplace* (Praeger, 1996).